THE
PAN AM
CLIPPER

Other titles in this series:

The Zeppelin, by Christopher Chant
The Orient Express, by Anthony Burton

THE
PAN AM
CLIPPER

The History of America's Flying Boats
1935 – 1945

ROY ALLEN

amber
BOOKS

This Amber edition first published in 2018

Copyright © Amber Books Ltd 2018

First published in 2000 as *The Pan Am Clipper*

Published by
Amber Books Ltd
United House
London N7 9DP
United Kingdom
www.amberbooks.co.uk
Appstore: itunes.com/apps/amberbooksltd
Facebook: www.facebook.com/amberbooks
Twitter: @amberbooks

ISBN 978-1-78274-604-1

Printed in the United Kingdom

Picture credits
Aerospace Publishing: 32–3, 53, 61 (m), 64–5, 69, 75, 84–5, 86–7, 88, 90(l), 91, 96(b), 97(b), 99, 104–5, 106 (both).
Roy Allen: 28–9, 96(t), 98–9. **Archives and Special Collections of the University of Miami Library**: 6–7, 9(t), 18–19,
21, 22 (both), 23, 27(t), 31, 34–5, 36 (both), 38–9, 39, 40–1, 44, 45, 46 (both), 47, 48, 56, 66, 67, 70–1, 72–3, 74–5, 76,
76–7, 80–1, 89 (both), 92–3, 94–5, 97 (m). **Boeing**: 90 (r), 93, 100–1, 101, 102, 103. **Hugh W. Cowin**: 8–9, 14–15, 24–
5, 26, 41, 64. **Getty Images**: 30(t). **Lockheed Martin**: 42–3, 50–1, 52, 54(b), 55, 58, 60, 61(t), 62–3. **Royal Aeronautical
Society**: 5, 27(b), 30(b), 57, 68 (both). **TRH Pictures**: 2–3, 10, 11, 12–13, 17, 20 (both), 54(t), 82 (both), 83, 85.

Contents

Pan American engaged in numerous joint airline operations in the beginning, invariably absorbing the partner
in due course. Pictured here is the Fokker VII and landplane operation.

CHAPTER ONE

Taking to the Air

The name of Juan Trippe has long ago passed into the annals of air transport history. This book is about the contribution he made to one slice of that history through his employment and development of a particular kind of aircraft – the flying-boat. Beginning with a collection of small amphibians, Trippe, through the medium of his airline Pan American World Airways, urged and supported the advancement of the water-based craft to the point where his fleet became the largest and most famous airliners in the world – the Pan American Clippers.

The reason why the water-based aircraft was adopted with such success is readily explained in the following account, but its service to travellers, governments and even heads of state had to be accompanied by a good share of business acumen, promotional skill and high regard for passenger comfort.

Juan Trippe and Pan Am put all of these ingredients together and produced a winning formula which is still talked about today. The Pan American Clipper flying-boats were the toast of international air travel, and a few remaining former passengers can testify to their comfort and unparalleled atmosphere of luxury.

It is hard to believe that the Clipper story occupied no more than 15 years in air transport history, and even more that it involved a total of just 100 aeroplanes, 25 of which were Clipper ships. Astonishing indeed, that what became the mighty Pan American World Airways grew out of this most successful period in its life with a fleet of 25 Clipper flying-boats.

Pan Am is gone now, and while relatively few people actually flew in their flying-boats, the world misses the excitement, the glamour and the technical wonder of the beautiful craft which contributed, ultimately, towards everyone flying.

Just how massive the international airline business would become was the stuff of crystal ball gazing in the 1920s, but the time was right for many because initial pioneering work had been done and the groundwork laid for more professional operations. When entrepreneur Juan Trippe entered the scene in 1923, the early disasters, wasted attempts and financial failures were generally out of the way and the scene set for a large dose of success.

Trippe was able to generate this success because he could produce everything that was required for a winning airline, but he was by no means the first on the scene. A number of tentative air services had been tried, but there had been no real attempt by anyone to maintain schedules. Credit must go to a group of businessmen and city officials in Florida for putting together the first company to operate a scheduled airline service as early as 1913. In December of this year, a contract was signed with the City of St Petersburg for a subsidy guarantee to help get the air company off of the ground. This was the St Petersburg– Tampa Airboat Line and flights were planned for the months of January, February and March 1914.

Tom Benoist was the manufacturer of the aircraft intended for the flight and, interestingly enough, his Benoist flying-boat

BELOW *The first of the water babies, this Sikorsky S-36 amphibian was operated by Pan American Airways on a trial basis.*

was just that – a small flying-boat designed for the task, with wings in the biplane fashion after the US aviation pioneers the Wright Brothers, with an extended rear fuselage carrying a tailplane and with a 75-hp engine driving a pusher propeller. (The Wright Brothers' original Flyer had a 12-hp engine, which illustrates how much progress had already been made).

There was perhaps a portent of things to come with this little flying-boat, for it was the vehicle by which the first scheduled air service in the world was made, between St Petersburg and Tampa, a distance of 18 miles (29km). The first airline flight took 23 minutes and the return flight just 20 minutes, and through January 1914 a regular timetable service was operated with two round trips a day. Most of its municipal subsidy was repaid in January and the Airboat Line was pretty well self-sufficient through February and March.

The contract expired on 31 March 1914 and operations were continued during April, but for a variety of reasons, including a fall in business, this pioneering service petered out and was shortly terminated.

All of this took place while Juan Trippe was still at school, and then came the years of World War I. With the end of the war in Europe in 1918, the Allied authorities were left with thousands of military aircraft that had outlived their usefulness. It was not long before companies were being formed to put to use some of these redundant military aircraft, which could be readily obtained as war surplus.

In the United States the St Petersburg–Tampa Airboat Line had demonstrated that air transport could be a practicable, safe,

ABOVE *The prime architect of the Pan American airline system, Juan Terry Trippe, seen here (left) with his technical adviser and friend, the famous Charles A. Lindbergh.*

and highly attractive business, and in Europe now aviators were anxious to confirm that it could be a profitable business too. The first scheduled international air service in the world was begun between London and Paris on 25 August 1919, by the company Aircraft Transport & Travel, and this company was soon joined by many others, the largest proportion of which were doomed to failure in a few short years.

In the United States, the technical development of aircraft that had been urged by the war years was increasingly being put to use by a new band of hopeful airline operators. One such company was Aero Limited, which made a series of flights in August 1919 between New York and Atlantic City, using war-surplus HS-2 flying-boats, and a little after this Florida West Indies Airways Inc operated some services in the Caribbean. Aeromarine Airways Inc was next on the scene at Keyport, New Jersey. During the winter of 1920–21, Florida West

ABOVE *The S-36 was quickly followed into service with Pan Am by the Sikorsky S-38, an eight-passenger amphibian with a 600-mile (960-km) range.*

Indies Airways began a successful experimental air-mail service between Key West, Florida, and Havana, Cuba, having received a government air-mail contract in October 1920. Aeromarine Airways absorbed this operation before long.

Another hopeful was the American Trans Oceanic Company which began services, from Miami to South Bimini in the Bahamas, on 20 December 1919, and the company operated a round trip daily service for two full winter seasons, charging $25 for the 50-mile (80-km) return flight. Then, on 1 November 1921, Aeromarine began two regular daily services between Key West and Havana and from Miami to Nassau, capital of the Bahamas. The Havana trip took two hours for the 105-mile (169-km) flight and cost $50 single. The Nassau service took two-and-a-half to three hours for 185 miles (298km) and cost $85 single. These services were operated by converted F-5L flying-boats, which had been built for the US military by the Glenn Curtiss Company, and converted for civilian use. These services by Aeromarine were operated throughout the winter of 1921 but were terminated on 1 May 1922.

In 1922, Aeromarine's services were increased in number and the route stretched to other points, including New York, Atlantic City and points in New England. As with so many,

however, Aeromarine did not live up to the promise that its operations appeared to offer, and in 1923 the company encountered financial difficulties and closed down. The Foreign Airmail Contract, which had been instituted by the US Post Office by way of objective encouragement, terminated also with the company's closure.

ENTER JUAN TERRY TRIPPE

In the summer of 1923, Juan Trippe and his friend John Hambleton joined as partners to form Long Island Airways. This was Trippe's first attempt at forming an airline, although it was not much more than an air taxi service. Together they purchased seven surplus navy seaplanes which they modified to carry two passengers on the flights between Long Island and nearby beach resorts. Long Island Airways lasted no more than two years, but it can be said to have blooded the partners for future airline adventures.

Juan Terry Trippe appeared destined to engage in airline adventures from the time of his school days. He was born in Seabright, New Jersey, on 27 June 1899 to a wealthy family. His father, Charles White Trippe, was a Wall Street investment banker and his mother's side of the family was wealthy also.

RIGHT *Charles Lindbergh has a final word with his boss, Juan Trippe, as he prepares for the first flight from Miami to Cristobal in 1929.*

Charles Trippe had many connections in the monied social circles, and the sons of his friends played with Juan or went to school with him.

At the turn of the century, aviation was literally brand new and Juan Trippe took an interest in it right from the beginning. The fast pace of change that has characterised aviation throughout its whole period was rapid even then, and by the time he was 12 years of age Juan Trippe was wildly keen to become involved in this fascinating new business – so much so that his father sent him to the Curtiss Flying School in Miami. Later, while at Yale in 1917, he joined the Naval Reserve Flying Corps, where he earned his wings as a pilot. After graduation it was not clear where he would go from there, but it was not long before Juan Trippe was putting his great interest to business use.

After Yale, Juan joined his father in a banking career in Wall Street. His friend John Hambleton, who also came from a banking family, was just as interested in aviation as was Juan Trippe. Their mutual interest led to Long Island Airways.

FLY THE MAILS

With time-saving in mind, and also perhaps the worthy thought that it should look towards the possibilities of the new technology afforded by air travel, the US Post Office requested bids for the carriage of US mail by air as early as June 1918. Shortly afterwards an Air Mail Service was instituted, initially using military pilots and surplus military aeroplanes, and later aircraft modified or built for the purpose.

This Air Mail Service had its successes and also had its difficulties, ranging from weather problems to technical delays and arguments over air safety. Nevertheless, some two-and-a-quarter million miles were flown during the period of the operation and some 14 million air-mail letters carried at a regularity of 94 per cent. However, 34 pilots lost their lives in the years to 1925: a high enough price to pay for this pioneering operation.

With its quite costly subsidy, the Post Office had never intended to operate the Air Mail Service on a permanent basis, and numerous voices were raised against it. One such voice was that of Clyde Kelly, the Congressman from Pennsylvania, who represented the railways. The railways argued that the Post Office should not be carrying its own mail. A reappraisal by the US government led to the Contract Air Mail Act, which was passed on 2 February 1925 and which was actually named the Kelly Act after Clyde Kelly who had argued for change.

LEFT *Lindbergh is seen again in the cockpit of one of the Fokker F-VIIs which were used on the original mail flights to Cuba, before the flying-boats became predominant.*

ABOVE *Against a backdrop of sea and boats, and with water all around, aircraft such as this Sikorsky S-38 amphibian fitted naturally into the scene.*

The Kelly Act provided for the transfer of air-mail services from the Post Office to private operators under a scheme of competitive bidding, for a period of four years. In essence, this meant that the Post Office would itself move out of the air-mail business and pay private operators to carry the mail, under what today would be called a public–private partnership. This Act was shortly followed by the Air Commerce Act, signed by President Coolidge on 20 May 1926, which was designed to designate and establish airways, to organise air navigation, to arrange for research and development, license pilots and aircraft and to investigate accidents. The first Air Commerce Regulations came into force on 31 December 1926, and with this the groundwork was laid for the development of the airline business in the United States.

Seeing the possibilities of this new development, Juan Trippe wasted no time and talked to as many of his former Yale friends as possible, persuading them to join him in putting up money for a new airline. There were plenty of friends he could talk to. Apart from John Hambleton there was Bill Vanderbilt, of the Vanderbilt family, and Cornelius V. Whitney. Each of

these contributed $25,000 towards the formation of Eastern Air Transport. This company was based in New York and proposed to bid for the New York–Boston air-mail rights. Another operator, Colonial Airways, was being formed in Boston for the same purpose, and believing that this company stood at least as good a chance of winning the contract as his own Eastern Air Transport, Trippe persuaded its backers to join forces with him.

Their new company, launched with capital of $300,000, was named Colonial Air Transport. The president of Colonial AT was General John F. O'Ryan and other distinguished men on the board included Governor John Trumball of Connecticut

and R. E. Cowie, president of the American Railway Express company. Trippe became vice-president and general manager and, in successfully bidding for the New York–Boston mail contract, Colonial AT obtained the first contract under the Kelly Act.

Operations began in December 1925 with Fokker Universal aircraft, but Trippe was anxious to fly passengers as soon as possible, for which modern, reliable multi-engined aircraft would be needed. When he met Anthony Fokker, the Dutch aircraft designer, on a trip to the United States in 1925, Trippe was impressed and took a great interest in him. Acting on his own initiative now, Trippe placed an order for two three-engined F.VII aircraft costing $38,000 each.

This did not square well with the other Colonial AT board members, who believed firmly that passenger-carrying should not yet be risked. Trippe and the other board members argued and in 1927 Trippe sold out of Colonial AT, together with his personal backers Cornelius Whitney and John Hambleton.

CARIBBEAN DREAM

Trippe was now a free agent again and together with his partners looked for a new airline opportunity. They concentrated on the New England area, but another group was looking with interest at the Caribbean. Trippe had previously flown down to Havana with Fokker, and thought that the area looked very promising for air services, as did Latin America. Former World War I flying ace Eddie Rickenbacker and his partner Reed Chambers had organised Florida Airways early in 1926, operating for about nine months between Atlanta and Miami, and they were also interested in the region. Rickenbacker himself had an impressive group of banking friends who had invested in his airline, including Percy Rockefeller, Charles Stone, Charles Hayden, George Mixter and Richard F. Hoyt (chairman of Curtiss-Wright) and others. They had always had an interest in operating a route to Havana, but Florida Airways had no good connections to the north. Before long the airline lost money and went into bankruptcy.

On another front a former young army officer, Captain J. K. Montgomery, had been looking at the idea of a trans-Caribbean air service and he interested bankers, including Richard D. Bevier and George Grant Mason, in the idea of an airline. They talked with President Machado of Cuba about services and incorporated a company, Pan American Airways Inc, in New York City on 8 March 1927. The formalities for the registration of this company were completed on 14 March 1927.

Elsewhere, Trippe was putting together a new operating company, the Aviation Corporation of America (AVCO), and on 2 June 1927 this company was registered with the three partners, Trippe, Hambleton and Whitney each putting up $25,000. They invited friends to put in capital up to a total of $300,000 – this sum was quickly subscribed, such was the power and range of Trippe's friends and contacts. Money came from wealthy friends such as William H. Vanderbilt, Edward O. McDonnell, Sherman M. Fairchild, of the Fairchild Airplane company, W. Averill Harriman, Grover Loening, William A. Rockefeller, John Hay Whitney and Seymour Knox, a member of the Woolworth family. This powerful group engaged a Dutchman, André Priester, as their operations expert. Priester had been partner to Anthony Fokker on his trip to the United States and he later became a key figure in Pan American Airways.

Three financial groups were therefore looking at the high stakes of Latin American air routes, with the important bonus of foreign air-mail contracts.

On 16 July 1927, the Key West–Havana air-mail contract was awarded to Montgomery's group, Pan American, but the contract was actually worthless because the company had not secured landing rights. Trippe's plan now was to pull all three groups together, and preliminary discussions began with Trippe's group proposing to put $300,000 into Montgomery's Pan American Airways. This investment was to represent 45 per cent of the capital of a new Pan American, while Montgomery's and Hoyt's (ex Florida Airways) groups were to subscribe the remainder. The discussions were far from smooth, one major impasse being the insistence of both Trippe and Hoyt having a majority holding in the new company. Finally, all three agreed on an equal $33\frac{1}{3}$ per cent interest, while in the event the proportions were some 40 per cent each for the Aviation Corporation of America and Florida Airways together with a 20 per cent holding subscribed by Pan American Airways. Hoyt was made chairman of the board of the holding company, while Trippe was put at the head of the operating unit. Other executives included Bevier, Mason and Whitney.

The group cemented itself together on 11 October 1927, initially with the new name Atlantic, Gulf and the Caribbean, but very shortly afterwards adopting the title Aviation Corporation of the Americas, a subtle change to the name of Trippe's AVCO. This became a holding company for the operating unit Pan American Airways Inc and its start-up capital was $534,000.

THE FIRST SERVICE

Trippe ordered three Fokker F.VIIs and all three aircraft were to be built as landplanes despite the high proportion of over-water flying associated with Pan American operations from the beginning. Indeed, at this time there were no modern marine aircraft of suitable size available in the United States but a special safety feature specified by Pan American for the F.VII was the provision of watertight compartments in the aeroplane's plywood wing, affording buoyancy in the event of ditching. The first aircraft to be used proved in fact to be a similar machine, the Fairchild FC2. This was pure fortune for Trippe as Pan American still had to obtain an aircraft of any kind to introduce the first service, which had to be made on 19 October 1927. For the United States, flights were to be made once daily weather permitting at the rate of $40\frac{1}{2}$ cents per pound of mail carried to Havana. Cuba was to pay a flat fee of $150 for each trip from Havana to Florida irrespective of the load carried.

As 19 October approached, Trippe was becoming desperate to obtain his first aircraft, or indeed any aircraft, for there was no sign of the F.VIIs. The problem was solved by the appearance at Key West of a single-engine Fairchild FC-2 seaplane belonging to the Santo Domingo operator, West Indian Aerial Express. This

ABOVE *Pan American bought no less than 39 S-38s, and these orders ensured that Sikorsky's production line was kept in good business.*

aircraft, named the *La Nina,* was able to carry the 30,000 letters to Havana and was hastily chartered by Trippe for the operation. The mail had arrived from New York by way of the Florida East Coast–Atlantic Coastline Railroads and was contained in seven sacks weighing 251lb (113kg). The pilot, Cy Caldwell, took off at 8 a.m. for the 105-mile (169-km) flight to Havana, taking one hour for the trip and returning to Key West that afternoon.

Thus began Pan American's air service. Nine days later it was followed by regular air-mail services on the Key West to Havana route. All this had been possible because, while the old Pan American Airways had gained the US mail contract, Trippe had personally obtained monopoly landing rights in Cuba from President Machado himself. These had been gained by Trippe on a specific flight to Cuba.

The origins of what was to become the mighty Pan American World Airways can now be seen. Trippe acquired an existing airline through the medium of financial power and, while he was positively interested in the region, in particular Cuba, he was presented with an officially authorised route for mail and passengers in a contract which had been awarded to somebody else. Trippe was to take this service on to great and remarkable things.

An S-38 was used to make the first Pan American air-mail flight to Paramaribo, in Dutch Guiana, in November 1930.

CHAPTER TWO

Down to the Sea

Juan Trippe was able to smile contentedly at the fact that he had become head of his own airline. At least it looked that way, for the air was still very rough for pioneering operators in the late 1920s and it would not be long before a financial catastrophe overtook the whole of America which would put many major companies out of business, let alone burgeoning airlines. But Wall Street was fading into the distance as he now set himself purposefully to developing a major airline. Many of his partners would depart in the years ahead, but many would stay with him as he continued to demonstrate that his thinking and his plans were right.

Having got off the ground, the new Pan American had to lay the foundations for further development. Ironically, in the years ahead it would be the business of taking off from water that would bring Pan Am its greatest fame and rewards for many years to come. Trippe intended to move quickly to consolidate his position in the Caribbean. Even before gaining the mail contract for services to Cuba, he had presented his company's directors with a plan for the airline which took it far beyond Havana from Key West. Trippe's idea was to develop a number of routes, one going from Miami to Cuba and then across to Mexico and to South America, and another extending down the chain of Caribbean islands to Trinidad. The United States would be linked by air to Valparaiso, Chile, and the company would attempt to gain landing rights in Cuba, Mexico, Costa Rica, Honduras, Guatemala, El Salvador, Peru, Chile and Venezuela.

For the initial service, the tiny island of Key West harbour was the initial base for Pan Am. This is the largest and most

ABOVE *The Sikorsky S-38 served Pan American well in the early days of water-borne operations, at a time when passenger numbers were small.*

westerly of the chain of islands known as the Florida Keys, which string out from the southern tip of Florida. A former US Army airfield, Meacham Field, was available, and a hangar, workshop and a tiny office building were erected there. The landing ground at Havana was to be the Cuban Army field of Camp Columbia. Following the first flight of 19 October 1927, the airfield at Key West was prepared for use and the first of Pan Am's own aircraft was delivered for service. Fitted for mail-carrying work, this was a derivative of the Fokker F.VII landplane. Powered by three 220-hp Wright Whirlwind engines these 80-mph (128-kmh) aircraft could carry eight passengers as an alternative load to the 1800lb (820kg) of cargo, or of course a combination of both. At that point single-engined transports were the usual type for airline services; the F.VII was designed to a high specification and was the first three-engined aircraft to enter service with a US carrier. Most of the fuselage and tail unit comprised a fabric-covered metal structure, wood being used in the construction of the wing.

ABOVE *Early production of the F.VII, showing how radically production methods would change over the years as materials developed from wood to metal.*

KEY WEST–HAVANA

The first revenue flight to be operated by Pan Am aircraft was made on 28 October 1927, and this is generally regarded as the airline's first scheduled flight since it marked the beginning of regular services proper on the Key West–Havana route. It was also the first regular international service by any US airline. In

command of the Fokker aircraft (called the *General Machado*) was chief Pan Am pilot Captain Hugh Wells. Taking off at around 8.30 a.m., the aircraft flew in clear air for the first half hour before running into a line of squalls. These had to be avoided as far as possible, and doing so involved much cloud dodging. With no visual ground references or radio navigation was difficult. On returning to Key West, Captain Wells insisted that the aircraft be equipped with radio which would permit constant communication with the ground; this was subsequently installed.

Trippe had always intended that passengers should be carried by Pan American as soon as the airline could do so, and on 16 January 1928 the first fare-paying passengers were flown between Key West and Havana, in both directions. That day seven were taken on the flight to Havana and four were flown to Key West. The initial one-way fare for the 80-mile (130-km) trip was $50, some 55 cents per mile. This in fact was a less healthy rate of revenue than the 40½ cents per pound US mail rate but in money terms alone it was still fair reward for the task. Each passenger could take 30lb (14kg) of luggage free of charge.

However, mail had priority and when the F.VII's 1800-lb (820-kg) capacity was wanted for mail carriage, passengers and other cargo could not be accommodated. In January 1928, the third month of operations, Pan American carried 23,393lb (10,620kg) of mail from Key West to Havana, an average of over 750lb (340kg) per trip; 1683lb (762kg) was carried in the reverse direction. A total of 71 passengers was flown between the two points during that month, together with 1572lbs (712kg) of cargo (mostly newspapers) and 631lbs (284kg) of excess baggage. One daily return trip was flown on this single Pan American route, and 75 minutes of block time (one way) was scheduled.

On 16 January, the single hangar at Key West was finally completed so that the three aircraft now in service, two C-2 versions of the F.VII, and one F.VII, could be accommodated, together with a single Sikorsky S-36 amphibian, which was the first in a long line of Sikorsky aircraft to be used by Pan American. Hangar shelter for the aircraft took them out of the sometimes bad weather and enabled the first in-house maintenance to be made.

The Sikorsky S-36 was the only version of its type to be built by the Sikorsky company and was operated by the airline on a two-month lease from the manufacturer, beginning on 7 December 1927. A twin-engined amphibian, it could carry seven passengers or 1800lb (820kg) of cargo and cruise at 90mph (145kmh). The aircraft was leased to Pan American for evaluation but was not proceeded with.

Although the matter had not been considered, provision of the S-36 gave Pan American its first experience of the water-borne operations that were shortly to play a major role in the airline's services to the Caribbean and elsewhere. As with all land aerodromes of the time, Camp Columbia in Havana could become a mess for wheeled aeroplanes in heavy wet weather and it was fortunate that this region had a good share of sunshine and hot dry weather throughout much of the year.

PAN AM SPREADS ITS WINGS

The new Pan American Airways was awarded every foreign air-mail route for which bids were invited. The company fitted exactly the concept of the US chosen instrument for overseas air-mail service, and with one exception all contracts were let for ten years at the maximum rate of $2 per mile. Trippe gained the security of foreign landing rights at almost every destination in which he was interested. Thus, Pan American was soon able to offer services from Miami to Cuba, Venezuela, San Juan, Santo Domingo, Port of Spain, Nassau, Mexico City, Cristobal, Montevideo, Buenos Aires, Santiago and other destinations in Chile. Within two years of operating, the new Pan American Airways established a comprehensive network around Central and South America, and by 1930 this network included Argentina, with an extended flight from Paramaribo in Dutch Guiana to Buenos Aires.

As far as the United States was concerned, Pan American continued to demonstrate its capability for continued operation of air services and indeed was extending and developing these services constantly. Without any formal statement to the effect, Pan American had become the chosen instrument for international air services to the region. Later it would literally become the US flag carrier to this and other parts of the world. This was not to say that US policy excluded other operators, but merely the government's preference for a carrier that was demonstrating its business skills and technical fitness for the role.

It is not difficult to understand the rise to eminence of the water-borne aircraft. The war in Europe had brought to that region great numbers of land aerodromes which, by the war's end, had been developed from nothing more than large fields to purposeful landing sites. These accommodated the military fighters and bombers and observation aircraft which carried on

BELOW *Resolute and authoritative, the captain of a Clipper Ship would keep his hands firmly on the control column for much of the flight, to physically guide the aeroplane.*

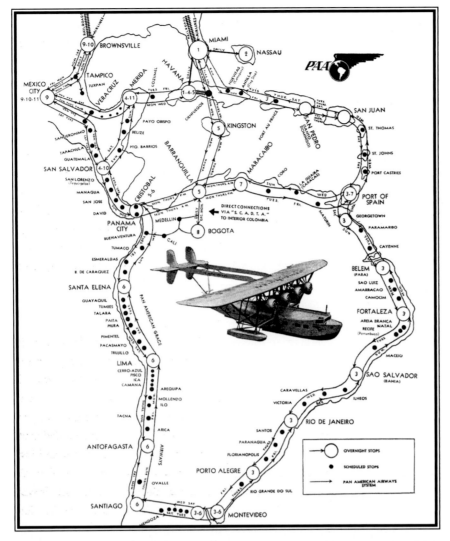

LEFT *PAA publicity map of the period showing the widening coverage of the Caribbean and South American services.*

their destructive tasks over the 1914–18 period and which had been large fields and open areas for the original European aviation experiments. The Wright Brothers had brought the aeroplane to Europe as a landplane and that was how it was viewed, with a few experimenters attempting flights from the rivers, such as the Seine.

There had been no such war and no such military aviation in the United States and consequently no purposely constructed landing grounds. Governments had put their money behind military aerodromes in Europe to provide for their new military craft (for which they had shown little or no interest prior to the war) and there was no such requirement in the United States. A number of enlightened towns or states had seen the potential for air services as a result of the US Post Office's air services, but the sum total of designated aerodromes in the whole of the United States in the 1920s was just over 1000.

The situation was worse in Central America and the Caribbean, with proper landing grounds being virtually non-existent. The practical necessities of a Caribbean service precluded the use of landplanes, as routes were either over water or across short stretches of land. In most of the countries of the Antilles, West Indies and Central America, landing grounds were mostly of the most primitive type or non-existent. In contrast, the building of harbours for flying-boats was relatively easy and both climate and water conditions were favourable. As Pan American's route network lengthened, so did its requirement for landing sites. Accordingly Pan American decided to concentrate its activities on the waterborne aircraft. The general view in the countries of the region was that if the United States wished to operate air services permission would be granted,

ABOVE *The interior of an S-38, illustrating the wonderful views that were enjoyed by passengers on these early flights.*

ABOVE *A truly memorable sight for those fortunate enough to experience it – the view from an S-42, somewhere over the Caribbean.*

but that was all that could be expected from local governments, many of which were generally impoverished and often corrupt.

Pan American's actions in this area were furthered by a development among the airlines which led to an early takeover and the acquisition of a new fleet for Pan American. In March 1929, a new company was formed in New York called the New York, Rio and Buenos Aires Line, or NYRBA, and this represented a direct challenge to the Aviation Corporation of the Americas. The head of the company was Captain Ralph O'Neill, a former World War I fighter ace and later a Boeing salesman in South America. O'Neill had seen the enormous potential for air transport in that transport-starved continent and had gone to New York to look for backers for his proposed airline. He found them in the form of an impressive collection of industrialists, which included Reuben Fleet of the Consolidated Aircraft Corporation, F. C. Munson of the Munson Steamship Line, W. B. Mayo of the Ford Motor Company, J. E. Reynolds of International Founders and Lewis Pierson of the Irving Trust Company. Pierson brought in his son-in-law Richard Bevier as vice-president, together with J. K. Montgomery. These three had been partners in the original Pan American Airways and had left when Trippe and the AVCO organisation took over their company and began the first flights to Cuba.

In July 1929, a proving flight was made with a Ford Tri-Motor to Buenos Aires and the first NYRBA scheduled service opened on 21 August 1929 from the Argentine capital to Montevideo. In September, a Buenos Aires–Santiago route was added for both mail and passengers. The journey took seven hours and fifteen minutes and was the first trans-continental air route in South America. Mail contracts were obtained by NYRBA from the governments of Argentina, Chile and Uruguay. In November of that year, authorisation was obtained from the Brazilian government to operate within that country; a week later a new route was opened from Buenos Aires to Asuncion, Paraguay. The former US Assistant Secretary of Commerce for Aeronautics, W. P. McCracken, became chairman of the board.

O'Neill bought Ford Tri-Motors for his services, three Sikorsky S-38 amphibians and six Commodore flying-boats from the Consolidated Aircraft Corporation, of which Reuben Fleet was the owner. While the Sikorsky S-38 was an adequate craft, seating eight passengers and offering the dual functions of land and seaplane at the handling point, the Commodore was an advanced new machine which would seat 22 passengers, and represented the first of a new breed of water-borne craft.

ENTER THE FLYING-BOAT

The Commodore was originally designed for naval patrol work by Fleet's company. It was a sizeable craft for its day, with a wingspan of 100ft (30m), a length of 68ft (21m) and overall height of 16ft (5m). It was powered by two Pratt & Whitney Hornet engines, each developing 575hp, and the gross weight of the aircraft was just under 18,000lb (8200kg). Its designed range was 1000 statute miles (1609km), and with a cruising speed of 100mph (161kmh) and a capability for carrying 22 passengers, the Commodore was, all-in-all, a fine craft. It was a product of the company founded by Reuben Fleet in May 1923, the Consolidated Aircraft Corporation.

Fleet was a self-made businessman with six years' experience in the US Army Air Service. Later, when war added to the demands for aeroplanes, Consolidated Aircraft Corporation was to become one of the largest aircraft manufacturers in the United States. Like the Trippe family, Fleet's forebears had their roots in England, and his father had reached the Pacific Northwest by way of Kansas City. After finishing school, Fleet entered the Culver Military Academy in Indiana, graduated in 1906, and for a brief period was a school teacher in Washington. He then started his own business and became a real estate dealer. With his first flight in 1914, he became an immediate convert to flying.

Fleet became a member of the Washington State Legislature and introduced a bill appropriating $250,000 for aviation training in the National Guard. The Bill died, but Fleet had attracted attention and was among 11 men to be chosen for pilot training in the scheme that had come from his Bill. He made his first flight from San Diego in 1917, and joined the military when the United States entered World War I in 1917. He left the Air Service in 1922, during which time he had made an impression on senior officers in the service.

He turned down jobs with aircraft makers William Boeing and Glenn Curtiss, and incorporated the Consolidated Aircraft Corporation in the State of Delaware on 29 May 1923. He gained a first order from the military for twenty TW-3 training aircraft, which on modification was renumbered the PT-1. A further contract for the PT-1 was placed in 1924, for fifty aircraft, at which point Fleet moved the production facilities to Buffalo, New York, where he took over a former Curtiss factory.

Further orders followed for training aircraft, for the navy as well as army, and by 1927 Consolidated Aircraft was making money. Further military designs followed, including a new bomber, the *Guardian*, which was a joint venture between Consolidated and Sikorsky, produced when Fleet and Igor Sikorsky had agreed to collaborate on what had been a Sikorsky design. Significantly, Sikorsky, a former competitor of Consolidated, came to play a more significant role with Pan American than did Consolidated. Indeed, Trippe was already using a fleet of Sikorsky S-38s by the time of the NYRBA challenge.

NRYBA was gaining ground in an area which Trippe had already been working hard to call his own, and on 18 February 1930, O'Neill launched the first through service between Miami and Santiago, using the east coast route via Brazil. In a great flourish of publicity he gained the services of no less than Mrs Herbert Hoover, the President's wife, to christen a Consolidated Commodore for this service. Having begun services with

BELOW *In its airline form, the Commodore carried a total of 22 passengers and cruised at 100mph (160kmh). It was used in the Caribbean.*

ABOVE *The S-42 was probably Sikorsky's finest flying-boat. It seated up to 32 passengers and cruised at 150mph (240kmh). This aircraft served with Pan Am until July 1946.*

NYRBA in November 1929, the Commodores had already been successful enough for O'Neill to increase his original order for six to fourteen. It might be said that the US Navy's loss was NYRBA's gain, for while the navy had turned down the Commodore, Fleet found a ready buyer for a commercial version of the aircraft in NYRBA – the airline in which Fleet was a major investor.

Both Consolidated and NYRBA came out well from this deal: it had a beneficial effect for Consolidated, for it provided work on the 14 aircraft, and the deal gave O'Neill an excellent aircraft for the South American services. The Commodores (whose naval name had been *Admiral*) had the capability for long ranges which resulted more from the shortage of adequate landing bases than from over-water crossings of great distance.

Trippe had strong political influence in the US Post Office Department, however, and conflict soon arose between NYRBA and Pan American. Pan American held the US mail contracts as far as Paramaribo, Dutch Guiana, and NYRBA found its path blocked for mail and passenger traffic across the gap from Port of Spain, Trinidad, along the chain of islands to Miami. Relations became strained and conflict continued and reached a critical point. The US Post Master General took issue with NYRBA's cut-price mail rates. The Post Master General made it clear that he would not award any US mail contract for an east-coast route to Buenos Aires to any other company than Pan American, and with so many countries in the region pledging exclusive allegiance to Pan American, NYRBA's economic problems mounted. Despite a high standard of operations, NYRBA passenger figures were as limited as its mail traffic and it was actually losing money on its operations.

Pan American did not itself receive US mail rights for the east-coast route until 24 September 1930, but preparations had

ABOVE *When Juan Trippe acquired a fleet of Commodores from the defunct NYRBA, 11 were already in service. The fleet was to total 14. This was the second to be delivered.*

been underway long beforehand and by mid-1930 traffic rights had been received from Brazil and the route had been surveyed as far as Rio de Janeiro.

It had been demonstrated that Trippe had more political clout in Washington and he had always satisfied the US Post Office in every regard. He had friends in powerful places and he moved in the highest circles, including that of the president. These facts aside, O'Neill's financial position deteriorated even further as NYRBA was losing heavily every month and running out of credibility with its investors. With political power being as important as money, Trippe knew that he was the most strongly placed for future air-mail contracts and he broached the idea of a takeover of NYRBA to O'Neill.

THE COMMODORES

O'Neill had been aware that he was out of favour with his investor friends and he had also shown himself to be a poorer businessman than Trippe through a number of actions, not the least of which was his low mail rates, which were sometimes half the officially recognised rate to that agreed between the United States and foreign governments. The board of NYRBA agreed to Trippe's proposal, and on 15 September 1930 the Aviation

Corporation of the Americas formerly acquired the assets of NYRBA including the fleet of 14 Commodore flying-boats. Pan American's pilots had cast envious eyes on the Commodores when they had first come upon the scene and now their own airline was to gain them as a fleet. For Pan Am, the day of the true flying-boat had dawned. They would carry a fast-growing number of passengers as well as the mail.

As NYRBA folded, Pan American took over the assets of the airline which included its subsidiary airline NYRBA do Brasil, which had been formed on 22 October 1929. This airline was to be renamed Panair do Brasil in October 1930 and a new chapter began in the development of civil aviation. Material assets aside, NYRBA's pilots were also given a new future as they were taken on by Pan American

The Commodores had cost O'Neill and NYRBA $100,000 each and now they were picked up at a low price by Trippe and Pan American. They joined Sikorsky S-38s on the major routes, in particular in to the Caribbean, with one of them starting the Kingston–Barranquilla service in December 1930. This 600-mile (965-km) long leg was probably the longest flown by any airline in the world at that time, and it shortened considerably the journey time from Miami to the US Canal Zone.

The Commodores were different aircraft again to the standard types of the period in that Consolidated had made a fine job of their interior quarters and replaced the uncomfortable wicker chairs previously used by upholstered seats fitted in

ABOVE *For aircraft that were made largely of wood, insects could present a very real problem in the hot and humid climes of Latin America.*

BELOW *For Pan American, first-class air travel in the 1930s meant the very best that could be offered in terms of luxury, comfort and service.*

three passenger compartments. These were reached by walking down a thickly carpeted centre isle. This was a quantum leap in comfort for passengers, who would be further attracted to flying when they travelled in the aircraft. On-board service had not reached the point where drinks and snacks were served, but flying in such new comfort was a delight in itself. The Commodore was said to be the first passenger aircraft to have upholstered seats.

The Commodores went on to give excellent service on the routes, almost all of which were in the Caribbean area. Pan American continued to use them throughout the 1930s and early 1940s and retired the last two of them in September 1946, after 16 years of service. Ironically, no more Commodores were taken by Pan Am after the 14-strong fleet, for Juan Trippe was concentrating his aircraft needs on Sikorsky, who came to play a much larger role in the development of Pan Am.

The growth in traffic in the region, both mail and passengers, was surprisingly marked and confirmed all that Juan Trippe and others had believed about its potential. The vast South American continent needed good, modern transport connections and Trippe intended to provide them. President Herbert Hoover oversaw the collapse of Wall Street and the onset of the worst economic depression the world had ever seen, but Pan American Airways flew on, building steadily. Juan Trippe's father was a casualty in this period, his bank going out of business.

Juan Trippe had financial troubles himself, and on several occasions had to turn to his investor friends to settle bills for his aircraft and meet a variety of debts.

Never, did Trippe lose confidence in himself or the future for Pan American.

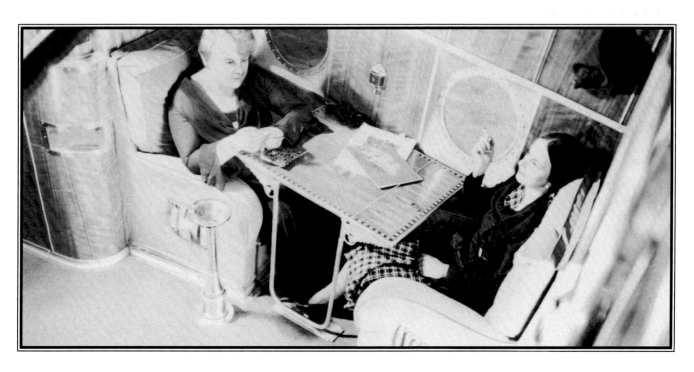

The family of Sikorsky flying-boats, including the S-42 shown here, formed the backbone of Pan Am's operations in the early years.

A Life on the Waves

Igor Sikorsky had had a very unprepossessing start to his life in America and his new aeronautical career. He came from a background similar in its way to that of Juan Trippe, but from the other side of the world. Born in Kiev in 1889 in what became the Soviet Union, Sikorsky's father was a professor, a lecturer and a writer and the family was comfortably off. As with so many young men of the time, Sikorsky was fascinated by aviation and by the early years of the twentieth century had become a leading aircraft designer, producing giant four-engined bombers for Russia at the time of World War I.

There was no room for aristocrats at the time of the revolution, however, even though they may have been leading engineering figures. Advised to leave Russia, Sikorsky decided to go to Paris. This he did by way of a circuitous route, moving to London first. He built five bombers for the French government, but with the ending of the war in 1918 his contract was cancelled, and there was little prospect for the services of an aircraft manufacturer when thousands of scrapped military aeroplanes had to be disposed of. The United States appeared to offer the greatest promise, and with the help of relatives and friends, who helped fund him, Sikorsky finally set sail for the States on 14 March 1919.

There was little work to be gained initially, but with borrowed money Sikorsky founded the Sikorsky Aero Engineering Corporation in March 1923. He built a few landplanes with little success and then the S-34, a two-engined amphibian. This was followed by the S-35, a landplane, and then the S-36, another amphibian.

LEFT *Charles Lindbergh is seen here with his wife, Anne Morrow Lindbergh, a pilot in her own right, who accompanied him on many survey flights.*

By now, Sikorsky was beginning to find his way around the operators of the fledgling airlines in the United States, and he came upon Juan Trippe. His S-36 amphibian was to be used by Trippe on a two-month trial basis but, like Trippe, Sikorsky was looking always ahead to better and more ambitious projects and he was turning to the S-38 in December 1927 just two months after Pan American's first revenue flight.

The first S-38 went into service with Pan American on 31 October 1928 in the Caribbean and was so successful that it was to become the backbone of Pan Am's fleet in the region. Powered by two Pratt & Whitney Wasp engines developing up to 450hp each, the S-38 seated just eight passengers, cruised at 110mph (176kmh) and most importantly was reliable. It had a 600-mile (960-km) range and its wheeled undercarriage gave the opportunity for ready handling on slipways and other landing points where facilities were primitive or non-existent for aero-marine craft. The S-38 could get bogged-down in shifting sand, but this was the price pioneers such as Trippe had to pay for airline operations until something better was devised. It was down to Pan American to improve the situation with marine bases and the airline undertook a sustained programme of developing bases around the island chain of the Caribbean.

This aircraft suited Trippe well. It did so well for Pan American, in fact, that Trippe ultimately bought thirty-eight S-38s at a cost of some $50,000 each. From the first delivery in 1928, deliveries continued until 1934, when the airline was better equipped with more Sikorsky models.

CHARLES LINDBERGH JOINS

The first of the S-38s was in service in January 1929 when Trippe obtained the services of Colonel Charles Lindbergh as technical adviser. After his famous solo trans-Atlantic flight to Paris, Lindbergh had become known the world over, and he had been invited to Mexico and a number of Central American countries to make a goodwill tour. He set off from Washington DC in December 1927, arriving back in St Louis two months later having visited every country bordering on the Caribbean and the Gulf of Mexico.

Trippe saw Lindbergh as much as an ambassador as a technical adviser, for he quickly came to demonstrate his worth to Pan American with his expert opinions and valued comments. With his knowledge and great foresight, the tall, curly-haired pilot became a great friend to Trippe, as well as a valuable member of the Pan American management. Much was gained by both out of what began as a business arrangement.

ABOVE *Igor Sikorsky built his career in providing Pan American with flying-boats but later turned to the helicopter, for which he became famous.*

For Trippe, Lindbergh's membership of the company was worth valuable publicity, because Lindbergh was inundated with job offers following his flight across the Atlantic in May 1927 and he was one of the most sought-after aviation men in the United States. For Lindbergh, Pan American meant good employment that required a strong technical input. Lindbergh was only too ready and willing to provide this input because Pan American was a fast-developing airline.

Trippe and Lindbergh proved to be soul mates in enthusiasm. Trippe gave Lindbergh free rein for his actions and Lindbergh made a deep and on-going contribution to the furtherance of the airline. Lindbergh later became a Pan Am board member and continued to serve and advise. The association lasted for the rest of Lindbergh's life until his death in August 1974.

In due course, Lindbergh met Sikorsky, and the two of them developed a mutual respect. Sikorsky was already working on new designs, for the promise was clear, that Pan American would be a ready recipient for his aircraft if he could produce the right machines. Lindbergh made a valuable input, for while Sikorsky was the technical man, following and introducing technical advances in this fast-developing art, Slim Lindbergh (as he was known) was the practised user of the end products and understood what the airline required of an aircraft.

PUSHING SOUTH

Strong in the Caribbean region was a transport company called the W. R. Grace Corporation, a shipping and transport firm that was also interested in aviation. It had its own embryonic airline which would operate on the west coast of South America. Grace blocked Trippe's path southward through Colombia, while Trippe in response blocked Grace's path northward through Panama. Further transport conflict arose when a compromise was reached between the two companies through the forming of Pan American–Grace Airways Incorporated (Panagra), with Grace and the Aviation Corporation of the Americas each contributing 50 per cent of the $1 million in stock. On 2 March 1929, Panagra was awarded a mail contract from the Canal Zone to Santiago and Buenos Aires and the difficulties for Pan Am were solved once again.

The S-38 fleet of amphibians, meanwhile, was flying around the region and developing the traffic for Pan Am. The little craft carried on the nose a winged globe with the letters PAA fronting the symbol. The legend Pan American Airways System was painted on the twin booms. Variations on the winged

BELOW *Every new business creates the need for a supporting industry. Aircraft maintenance called for specialised equipment, such as working frames to reach the aircraft.*

globe were made over the years, the letters PAA later being incorporated into the half wing. By 1928, Pan American had carried 9500 passengers and had flown 129,335 revenue miles (207,000km). In 1929, mail and cargo were still the dominant loads but passenger traffic doubled in this year to a total of 20,728 passengers, while the aircraft miles flown increased to no less than 2,752,880 miles (4,404,600km). By now some sixty air bases were owned or operated into by Pan American and Panagra; 25 ground radio stations were in operation.

The volume of traffic carried was considered less than satisfactory, however, in the light of the volume of revenue miles flown, which pointed to the need for a more productive aeroplane than the S-38. The S-38 was a fine aircraft for water

operations, but what Pan American now needed was an aircraft that could do a proper job in handling the volume of traffic which was clearly there to be gained.

Listening to what Lindbergh had to say about the matter, Trippe turned to Sikorsky for his latest design, the S-40 flying-boat. The S-40 carried a crew of six and 38 passengers, or almost five times the number of the S-38. Trippe ordered three. The S-40 was to be powered by four Pratt & Whitney Hornet engines and was easily the largest US civil aircraft of the era. The aircraft was scheduled for delivery in 1931 and would cost $125,000 each.

Before the aircraft was to join the fleet, however, the NYRBA takeover had occurred and the Commodore fleet had

come into use. As there were 14 Commodores, Pan American was adequately served until the arrival of the S-40s, which would be more capacious and superior craft.

Meanwhile, Trippe went on expanding his network and acquiring other airlines that represented a threat or were generally irritants. One such airline was a company called SCADTA (Sociedad Colombo–Alemana de Transportes Aereos), an airline in Colombia managed by a Dr Paul von Bauer. For some time SCADTA gave Trippe a lot of trouble through its Colombian operations, but in 1931 the Aviation Corporation of the Americas acquired 84 per cent of the SCADTA stock. Pan Am thus had controlling interest and the way was open for its through-route down the west coast.

ABOVE *By 1934, Trippe's airline was now calling itself* Pan American Airways System. *The S-42 seen here,* West Indies Clipper, *was to be renamed twice.*

Other airlines acquired along the way were CMA of Mexico, CAT in Central Mexico, LAMSA in the same region and Compania Nacional Cubana de Aviacion Curtiss SA, which Trippe bought outright in May 1932.

With most of the loose ends tied up, Trippe now had freedom for the operations he needed in the region, and with mail contracts providing financial stability he was able to concentrate on developing better equipment for both passengers and mail. It was to be passenger traffic that particularly interested Trippe.

The S-42 enjoyed the status of being the best flying-boat in Pan American's fleet – until the arrival of the improved M-130.

South American Conquest

When considering the Sikorsky S-40 as a new model for the fleet, Trippe took into consideration a number of ponderables, not the least of which was whether the aircraft should in fact be a landplane. Nothing had changed where the provision of airports and air bases was concerned, this being the responsibility of airline operators or governments which might be subsidising them. Such subsidies were a way of life among a number of foreign airlines operating to the region, such as French and German operators, who were greatly backed by their governments.

Trippe noted that the marine base presented a number of problems. It meant for one thing that both passengers and equipment had to be transported across sometimes choppy stretches of water to the anchored aircraft riding the waves, which could mean handling problems. Not all flying-boat bases could be located in calm inlets, for these were tidal waters, frequently in undeveloped areas.

On the other hand, the few facilities required for the marine base were fairly basic and readily provided, whereas locations for land aerodromes were not readily to hand and did not automatically mean nice flat stretches of ground on which aircraft of steadily increasing weight could land. Heavy rains could also turn compacted stretches of ground into muddy fields and sometimes dangerous sites, and Pan American routes, in any case, were over long stretches of water. The flying-boat was the ideal aircraft for the task: it could land on the water and float while the landplane could put down nowhere except a totally suitable land spot.

LEFT *Charles Lindbergh (centre) was seen by Trippe as a valuable ambassador for the airline because of his international fame.*

BELOW *While the 1930s was a time of economic depression, many new construction marvels were introduced. The airline flying-boat and the Golden Gate Bridge, San Francisco, seen here partially built, were two such innovations.*

The water-based aircraft was favourite and the Sikorsky design with its greater capacity and true flying-boat characteristics marked it as a good choice. The S-40 was to be the first of the Clipper Ships.

DEVELOPMENT OF THE S-40

With Trippe's firm interest, Sikorsky began construction and development of the S-40. In appearance, the aircraft resembled a scaled-up S-38, but it was in fact a very different craft. For example, it had four engines that were mounted on a high wing, which was externally braced by horizontal cross braces linking the fuselage. The ensemble was held together by a collection of subsidiary struts and wires. Like the S-38, the twin fins and rudders were mounted on long booms extending from the rear of the wing. The boat-like fuselage was joined on either side by two large floats secured to the horizontal braces. All of this was to constitute an aircraft with a wing span of 114ft (35m), an overall length of 77ft (23.5m), and a height of 24ft (7.3m). The gross weight of the aircraft would be 34,000lb (15,436kg) at take-off and the range of the aircraft would be 900 statute miles (1440km).

The construction of the hull was in metal duralumin and riveted sheets of metal were in Alclad. The wing was fabric covered and its overall area measured 1740ft² (162m²). The tailplane area covered 461ft² (43m²).

The total fuel capacity of the aircraft was 1040 gallons (4763 litres). There were four fuel tanks in the wings, while the pontoon floats each carried another 250 gallons (1136 litres). The engines could be fed from any fuel tank, and all the fuel lines and valves were placed outside the cabin area to minimise the risk of fire and also to allow passenger smoking.

The S-40 was a flying-boat but, in continuance of the practice of ramp and slipway handling at the marine bases, the aircraft was given a set of retractable wheels. A smaller retractable wheel was fitted at the rear of the hull, which also served as a rudder when lowered by the pilot for steering the aircraft in taxi.

The S-40 was the best equipped aircraft Trippe had yet had for marine operations. Apart from the usual life jackets, inflatable rafts and other survival gear it carried more than 1.5 tonnes of anchors, mooring gear and emergency radios.

The interior finishing was also the best Trippe had ever had, partly because he specified so. The aircraft could carry up to 38 passengers and Trippe had every intention of providing them with the best in airline comfort they had yet experienced. To this end, two suites were arranged for passengers immediately aft of the cockpit, and these were what might be called first-class cabins. Each was separated by the main aisle. To their rear were three standard compartments, each with eight passenger chairs, upholstered in blue and orange. The seating was arranged in a four-abreast layout, with each seat having its own electric light, individual ashtray and cigarette lighter. Metal-mesh overhead racks were fitted for hand baggage.

Throughout the cabin section the finish was of the highest standard. Trippe felt that he was in a competitive business and that there would be emulators of this type of service before long, and he wanted to be talked about as providing the best, at least among his passengers. Polished walnut panelling on walls and bulkheads was set off by blue carpet laid throughout the passenger areas. Each compartment was large and spacious, and had high ceilings with large square windows that could be opened in flight. Overhead lighting added to the attraction and there were blinds to pull across the windows if passengers felt so inclined. In each cabin section there were pictures of the S-40 on the walls. Directly behind the lounge area there were two toilets and a compartment for mail and baggage. Further to this there was provision for the preparation of hot meals on board, which was almost certainly a first for Pan American in the expanding international airline business.

Five water-tight bulkhead doors were fitted for when the S-40 was over water, each of these doors having a porthole in the manner of an ocean liner. These were intended to give a feeling of greater security to the passengers.

Sikorsky had tested various hull shapes prior to construction of the S-40, trying several shapes before he was satisfied with that to be incorporated into the aircraft. Trippe had placed orders for the large, twin-boomed aircraft on 20 December 1929 and development and construction proceeded through 1930, until in April 1931 the aircraft was readied for test flights.

TESTING TIMES

The aircraft was taxied out into Long Island Sound and the engines revved. These four 575-hp Hornet engines hung below the S-40's top wing and each drove two bladed propellers. The aircraft was designed to fly and climb with its load on any three engines and maintain altitude on just two. Now, Sikorsky's test pilot, Captain Boris Sergievsky revved the engines to take-off speed and in a mile-long run lifted the aircraft into the air amid a shower of water. He would not have heard the onlookers' cheers that accompanied this event. The test flight was carried out to Sergievsky's satisfaction and in due course the aircraft was levelled off and tentatively brought home. The landing speed on the water was 60mph (96kmh).

More flights were carried out, and in the usual way of test-flying, various combinations were tried and numerous parameters established. The aircraft was flown on all four engines and just two engines. It was climbed to its intended cruising altitude of 13,000ft (3900m) and flown at different speeds and at different weights. Basil Rowe, who had been the owner of West Indian

ABOVE *Entry to the S-40 and S-42 passenger cabins could be a somewhat precarious business, with passengers negotiating their way across floating pontoons and a protective airbridge.*

Aerial Express and had joined Trippe when he sold out to Pan American, joined the S-40's test flight programme and with Charles Lindbergh made his own expert contribution.

The aircraft was considered ready for delivery by early October 1931, with all testing completed, and Rowe flew the aircraft to Washington DC, where Mrs Herbert Hoover christened the aircraft on 12 October, as she had christened the Consolidated Commodores just under two years earlier.

Before a crowd of several thousand, the president's wife christened the plane *American Clipper,* breaking a bottle of sea water over its nose. Resplendent in a blue-painted hull, the aircraft sported the now-familiar half-wing and globe and the letters PAA and also the aircraft's name. This was the first Pan American aircraft to bear the name of *Clipper,* which would become a registered trademark of Pan American. It was, in fact, the first of the Pan Am Clipper Ships. Trippe had conceived the title for the fleet and for future aircraft joining

it. His Clipper Ships were named after the China tea trade Clipper Ships of the 1860s, which had been the fastest of their day. Another corporate legend was added in due course to company notepaper: *The System of the Flying Clippers.*

Trippe was ebullient and his joy and enthusiasm shared by his officers and partners and all of the team now working for this high-flying airline. Beginning just a few years earlier with a handful of pilots and staff, Trippe now had several thousand people working for him who would know that the airline was making sense, and not destined for oblivion like so many others. In these difficult years, everyone was getting paid, for a service that was clearly wanted.

That year 316,859lb (143,853kg) of newspapers, parcels, air mail and other cargo was carried together with, most importantly, 45,579 passengers. The aircraft mileage had risen to over 5 million miles (8 million km). Perhaps the best achievement to be carried away from the christening ceremony by Trippe and others was the recording of the first annual profit in Pan Am's history, of $105,452 on revenues of $7,913,587. This excellent result reflected the professionalism that was going into Pan Am on all fronts, ranging from the use of facilities on

ABOVE *Women travellers were to discover that airline flying required new thinking about dresswear, and that picture hats could present serious problems.*

the Latin American system, on the aircraft maintenance front, and in ticketing, passenger handling and operations generally. The S-40 would carry the airline onward.

THE S-40 IN SERVICE

The *American Clipper* took off on its inaugural flight on 19 November 1931 bound for the Panama Canal Zone. For the first time, passenger luxury was matched by a new standard of operational activity. There was a captain in command rather than a pilot and he had a first officer as his co-pilot, a radio officer and a flight engineer, previously known as the mechanic. The steward (later called the purser) assisted the passengers and answered their needs with refreshments from the galley.

Trippe had said that his aircraft should operate like ocean liners and to this end the nautical theme was carried on throughout. The nautical terms 'port' and 'starboard' were introduced, and the crew were given naval-style uniforms. Pan American pilots, navigators and radio officers already wore blue uniforms with ranks designated by stars on the wings. Bold rings would be added later on the sleeve cuff and braid on the peak of

the caps. The steward's uniform consisted of dark trousers and a white, waist-length jacket with a white shirt and black tie. Apart from serving refreshments to the passengers it was the steward's job to point out scenic attractions through the windows to further the general wonders of air travel. He also dealt with official paperwork including customs forms.

On one of the flights from Miami to Havana, a particular first was achieved by Pan Am when they presented a film show, with the steward (or purser) working the projector. This experiment went on to last several months and was then dropped. It can be said to have been the first attempt at showing in-flight films.

Pan American's S-40s, together with the acquired fleet of Commodores, were furthering the attractions of travel to a growing band of passengers, while these increasing numbers were keeping the cash register ringing and establishing Pan American Airways as an airline to marvel at.

On the inaugural flight of 1931, Charles Lindbergh was in charge as captain and Basil Rowe his first officer. The aircraft stopped at Norfolk, Savannah, Charleston and Jacksonville and 32 passengers were taken on board at Miami's Dinner Key, including Igor Sikorsky. The flight was made from Miami to Kingston, Jamaica, then on to Barranquilla, and then Cristobal in the US Canal Zone. The first overnight stop was at Kingston, where Lindbergh and Sikorsky attended a dinner that evening to mark the occasion. The following day the flight departed for Barranquilla, which represented a 600-mile (960-km) stretch over open water. The S-40 reached Cristobal on 22 November where the crew and passengers were ceremoniously greeted and the Post Master of the Canal Zone accepted the mail.

A Skilful Operation

During this remarkable time, Pan American sailed on and passenger traffic continued to grow. In other regions of the world air traffic development could be more easily understood, for the great nations of Europe, Great Britain, France, Holland, Portugal and so forth had their empires or colonies to serve and their nominated airlines did the job with a guaranteed traffic. In South America, Pan American had to win the favours of businessmen, diplomats, civil servants and nationals of various countries looking for speedy and comfortable transport between destinations.

The second S-40 was delivered on 16 November 1931 and named the *Caribbean Clipper,* its registration number being NC81V and its construction number 2001. Identical to its predecessor, the one notable change was in the cost, for this had risen to $136,000 for a variety of reasons, including cabin improvements and refinements to flight deck equipment.

The last of the three, named the *Southern Clipper* was delivered to Pan American on 30 August 1932, at which point Trippe took the unprecedented step of ordering even larger flying-boats from Sikorsky, to be called the S-42. The S-42 would weigh more than 20 tonnes and would carry a similar number of passengers over even longer ranges at even higher speeds.

The three S-40s went on to accumulate many flying hours in the Caribbean. Most of the time they operated at 80 per cent loads and were a great commercial success for Pan American. On-time arrival was said to average 99 per cent. Comfort was a major factor, and the aircraft was advertised as the 'Pullman of the Skies', serving to put Pan American firmly on the map, with flights being booked weeks in advance.

BELOW *The thrill of a take-off from water was one of the high points of Clipper Ship travel.* American Clipper *was the first S-40 to bear the title of Clipper Ship.*

ABOVE *Sikorsky's flying-boats were being steadily improved.*
The Caribbean Clipper *was the second S-40 to be delivered in*
November 1931.

A service was introduced between Port of Spain and Caracas with stopovers at various small coastal towns in between. For Pan Am, operational experience on such trips was being gained all the time, in handling, refuelling and ministering to the varying needs of passengers. Aircraft maintenance was similarly being learned on the job, with a long supply line for spares stretching back to Miami. For the flight crew and growing band of engineers this was producing a professionalism that other airlines would find hard to match in the years to come. The Clipper Ships were Pan Am's symbol of air transport luxury, but behind their operation was an increasingly skilled organisation.

In the mid-1930s, the three S-40s were fitted with new and more powerful engines, four 660-hp Hornet models, which increased the range to 800 miles (1280km). This enabled the gross weight to be increased and the payload raised to carry even more cargo.

The three Clippers continued to operate in the Caribbean area until 1940, when they were retired from scheduled service with Pan American. With the onset of the war with Japan, the three S-40s were taken over by the US Naval Air Transport System and used as flying classrooms. In due course, the US Navy scrapped the *American Clipper* in 1943, and the *Caribbean Clipper* was retired in April 1943 to be finally written off in August 1944. The last of the three, *Southern Clipper* continued to fly until November 1944, when it too followed its predecessors to the scrap heap.

In total, the three S-40s logged over 10 million air miles (16 million km) during their career. They brought a new standard of travel to the American public and taught Pan American a great deal about aircraft operation. As the first of the Clipper Ships they made a proud and valuable contribution.

The first Martin under construction. Still on the horizon, the Martin M-130 would embody many new technical developments.

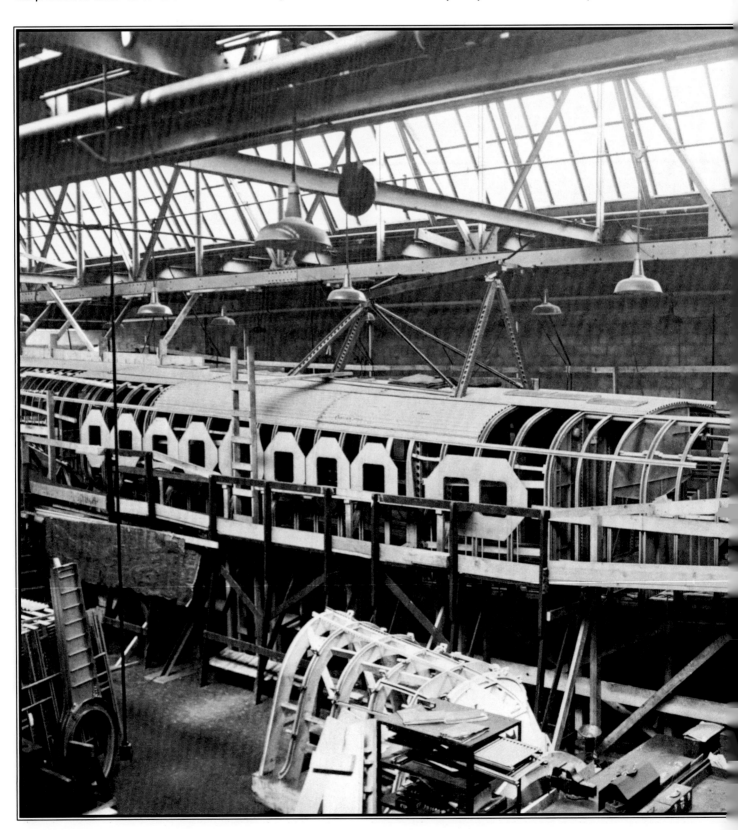

CHAPTER FIVE

Eyes on the Pacific

With much of South America and the Caribbean having been covered in his air network, Trippe's eyes were turning to other directions, to other parts of the world. Much consolidation work remained to be done in South America, and this was made in a variety of ways, but Trippe had always seen his airline as a fully international one, serving the major destinations of the world and not confined to US local activities. He did not, for example, wish to enter the competitive battles for domestic mail contracts in the United States, preferring to leave them to other airlines, of which there was a growing number.

Trippe had always been interested in the idea of a trans-Atlantic service, and such a service appeared highly attractive and a lucrative proposition. The massive body of water that constituted the North Atlantic, however, presented a formidable challenge and Trippe was well aware that the time was not right for this. Lindbergh, Pan American's technical adviser, could smile wryly when the subject arose for if anyone knew about flying the North Atlantic he did. He had flown the 'Big Pond' solo in 1927, and knew that a great deal would be required in the way of aircraft, communication links, diversionary alternates and so forth before scheduled services could be introduced.

He recalled that one of the more fanciful schemes being proffered at the time of the S-38 early operations was the trans-Atlantic Seadrome, this concept being devised in all seriousness by a company called the Armstrong Seadrome Development Company. The Seadrome constituted a large platform, resembling an aircraft carrier, which would be positioned at various intervals in the North Atlantic for the purpose of allowing versions of aircraft such as the S-38 to land and refuel. Seadrome platforms were to be mounted on massive piles sunk deep through the waters of the North Atlantic and equipped on the upper surface with full terminal facilities for air passengers, who might well have been wondering when another aircraft might be along to transport them to the next Seadrome in the event of their first aircraft breaking down.

THE PACIFIC BECKONS

A next logical stage of development would seem to be a network of services across the Pacific, from the West Coast of North America. This was a similarly massive ocean, and as a first step exploratory flights to Alaska might be made, the idea being that Asia could be reached from Alaska by way of Siberia, the Kurile Islands and Japan. Lindbergh had such a concept in mind, and undertook to make a survey flight into Alaska and the region.

Developments meanwhile were taking place in Central and South America serving to establish Pan American's position further in that region. Between the time of the Sikorsky S-40s and their first delivery and introduction into service, Pan American had ordered three of another Sikorsky type, the S-41 amphibian, a slightly enlarged version of the successful S-38. This had accommodation for 11 passengers and a cruising speed of 105mph (170kmh). These aircraft were to supplement the S-38s in service and, with the addition of fuel tanks in the wing floats with a capacity of 170 US gallons (645 litres), they would carry ten passengers over 800-mile (1288-km) stages. Developed over 1929–30, the S-41 was really an S-38 variant and used by Pan American in limited operations. Only seven were built.

Over this period, Pan American acquired a large number of different types of aircraft, many of which were landplanes and which frequently resulted from the outright acquisition or majority purchases of stock in various airlines in the region. As an example, in April 1932 Pan Am acquired 54 per cent of voting stock of Uraba, Medellin and Central Airways Inc (UMCA), a new Colombian carrier, which had been founded to operate between Medellin and the Canal Zone. In May 1932, Pan Am bought the entire stock of Nacional Cubana de Aviacion SA (Cubana), which operated a 749-mile (1206-km) long network within Cuba. Another subsidiary was established in Mexico to operate from El Paso to Mexico City and Mazatlan. This was Aerovias Centrales SA.

As aircraft of Pan Am's own choosing were gradually introduced, the disparate fleet was rationalised, and as the future projected network was based on flying-boat operations, Trippe decided to concentrate on these types and to make strong provision for the Latin American system while investing in the development of trans-ocean services in other regions.

It was possible for substantial investment to be made, in spite of the fact that the US Depression was at its worst, because Pan American was earning good profits. In 1932 it had made its most handsome profit so far, $698,526 on a revenue of $8.4 million. By the end of that year no fewer than 61 ground radio stations were operated by the airline in 27 different countries and there were now almost 2000 employees on the books.

Air travel in Latin America was by no means cheap. Indeed, it was regarded as expensive when compared with the cost of travel on US domestic air services, for Pan American's fares, at some 10 cents a mile on average, were almost double that of the charges for US domestic flights. The $500 air fare for a one-way trip between Miami and Rio de Janeiro, for example, was almost $200 higher than the comparable boat fare. However, for businessmen making a 10,000 mile tour of major South American cities, this could be achieved in six weeks by air instead of six months using surface transport. The saving in time and hotel expenses therefore far outweighed the extra expense of air tickets.

RIGHT *Captain Musick and First Officer R. O. Sullivan by the* China Clipper *before leaving San Francisco for Manila with the first trans-Pacific air mail. Trippe, under the tailplane, looks towards the pilots.*

BELOW *In characteristic stance, Lindbergh and Trippe consider their next move. Behind them is one of the small landplanes used by Pan Am subsidiaries.*

NORTH TO ALASKA

Air services in Alaska had begun as early at 1924 on local flights with a single-engined aeroplane. Trippe had visited the country as early as 1926 and thought there must be tremendous potential for air services in the region. In due course this proved to be so. By 1932 there were two large carriers operating, Alaskan Airways and Pacific International Airways Inc, which were both US financed. Losses were mounting at a dangerous rate, however, and before long Trippe intervened to offer his services. A Pan American subsidiary, Pacific Alaska Airways, was formed and in due course purchased both Alaskan Airways and Pacific International Airways. Once again Pan American acquired a motley collection of single-engined aircraft, together with all the operating bases and other equipment owned by the carriers. A new runway and airbase were established at Fairbanks, in central Alaska, and in 1933, in its first

full year of operations, Pacific Alaska Airways brought a new level of air service to local travellers.

The end point of Lindbergh's survey flight to Alaska and the Orient was the possible establishment of an air route to mainland China. It was not clear what aircraft would be used for this particular service, or precisely how it was to be conducted, but these and other questions were to be answered by the survey. On the flight, Lindbergh would not be alone: his wife, the remarkable Anne Morrow Lindbergh, served as navigator, radio operator, general helper, companion and all-round assistant. A pilot in her own right, Anne Lindbergh took her turn at piloting the aircraft on stages while her husband slept. Later she wrote a book about the flight, *North to the Orient,* in which she described the survey in graphic terms, demonstrating another talent, that of a fine writer.

Having flown a Lockheed aircraft for the first time in 1929, Lindbergh expressed his interest in owning a high-performance, low-wing monoplane for his own personal use to Jerry Vultee, then Lockheed's chief engineer. This was at the time of the National Air Races in Cleveland, and Vultee undertook to adapt the *Explorer,* a Lockheed design that had been a development of the record-breaking and highly successful Lockheed Vega. To suit Lindbergh's preferences the new aircraft would have a number of modifications, including a slightly smaller wing span and reduced area. Its low wing would be given two degrees of dihedral to improve handling characteristics. Lindbergh was happy with the proposed modifications, but requested that Vultee keep the cost of the aircraft down to that of the standard Vega. This proved to be $17,825. Even then Lindbergh had planned a number of survey flights, and this aircraft, named the Sirius, would now be used for the Alaska–China trip. The

aircraft was powered by a single 450-hp Pratt & Whitney Wasp engine and there would be accommodation for the pilot and one passenger in open tandem cockpits. With considerable foresight, Anne Lindbergh suggested that a sliding canopy be fitted over the tandem cockpits and this improvement was made. The aircraft was completed and flown in November 1929 and the Lindberghs took delivery of the aircraft in April 1930.

In preparation for the survey flight to Alaska and beyond, the engine was changed to a more powerful 575-hp Wright Cyclone, and then in 1931 it was fitted with twin floats for water landings. By removing the fuselage tanks and installing fuel tanks in each float, total fuel capacity was raised substantially for the long flights ahead. The aircraft was thus loaded up and started on the long flights to Canada, Alaska, the North Pacific and China. The Lindberghs set off on 27 July 1931 from New York, flying on to Ottawa and over the Canadian wilderness to Hudson Bay and the Arctic Circle. A flight was then made to Barrow, Alaska, and then to Nome in the Bering Strait.

In due course the Lindberghs reached the USSR, the Kamchatka Peninsular, and the Kurile Islands. From Tokyo they crossed the East China Sea to China and then on to Shanghai. They continued their journey on to Nanking and Hankow in China.

Hankow proved to be the end of the line, as the Yangtze River was in flood. In order to protect it from the waters,

LEFT *The S-42 provided the first opportunity for a galley where high-quality meals were prepared from the best food that could be kept unrefrigerated.*

BELOW *The recipients of these meals enjoyed their food together with a wonderful view from the windows (which in the future would become smaller and smaller).*

ABOVE *The arrival of the* China Clipper *in the Pacific. With the start of trans-Pacific services, warm South Sea hospitality was enjoyed by passengers and crew.*

Lindbergh requested the captain of the British aircraft carrier *Hermes* that the Sirius might be lifted on to the deck. This was done, but the following morning the aircraft was badly damaged while it was being lowered back into the river, the end result being that the aircraft was unflyable in its present form and had to be shipped back to Burbank.

The following year Lockheed rebuilt the aircraft as a landplane and it was returned to the Lindberghs. For their next survey flight a more powerful engine was fitted and the twin floats were re-installed.

While the survey flight to Alaska and the Orient of 1931 ended in catastrophe, it had accomplished its objectives and revealed many things, not the least of which was the fact that the Great Circle route could be flown but threw up more problems for scheduled airline operations than perhaps it was worth. Unpredictable and extremely severe weather conditions, the lack of adequate facilities and difficulties of communication were just a few of the problems. International politics added to the difficulties with no governmental relations between the United States and the Soviet Union, which meant that necessary landing rights in Siberia would not be granted so long as the United States continued to refuse official recognition of the USSR. For the time being at least, Trippe would have to content himself with operating internal Alaskan services. He set about doing this in 1932.

THERE MUST BE ANOTHER WAY

Trippe kept a globe in his office and studied this frequently, reportedly plotting routes and measuring distances with pieces of string. Wherever he looked there was water, and while it was possible to fly around the edge of the vast oceans such as the Pacific and North Atlantic, the idea of direct air routes across these oceans was the most attractive. In 1933, however, the technical and operational problems were too formidable. As in so many areas of aviation, Trippe was ahead of his time in knowing that in the years ahead such services would be possible, and long, over-ocean scheduled services could probably even become routine.

For the moment, Latin America and the Caribbean provided the bulk of traffic for Pan American's services and required even better aircraft. In this respect Sikorsky was not disappointing. The relationship that had developed between him and Trippe, Lindbergh and others with the S-38 and S-40 had grown even stronger and culminated in the S-42 in 1934 which would come to be judged as Sikorsky's finest flying-boat.

One of the reasons why only three S-40s were built and used by Pan Am was the deliberations taking place between Trippe and Sikorsky in 1932 even as the last S-40 was being constructed. Talks were concentrated on the S-42, which would be a much bigger aircraft and a true flying-boat. Longer-range capability was what Trippe sought in particular and he got this with the 1200 miles (1900km) performance of the S-42 which was a 30 per cent improvement on the S-40. Ideally, Trippe would have liked a capability for over 2000 miles (3220km), but the

suspended, while the wing itself was supported by two sets of V-braces on either side. The tailplane was mounted at the end and on top of the 68-ft (20-m) long fuselage, with twin fins and rudders mounted on top. Both the tailplane and fin and rudder combinations were braced.

The pilots' compartment was mounted high at the nose in the manner of a bridge, and passengers stepped down into the bowels of the cabin to reach their luxuriously appointed interior. Technically, the S-42 incorporated many new refinements, such as large wing flaps, extensive flush riveting, engine synchronisation indicators, propeller brakes and automatic carburettors. The aircraft's wing loading was the highest to date, at 28.5lb per ft^2 (137kg per m^2). Had

engine manufacturers, like Sikorsky, were working at the edge of technology and the aviation business still had to make haste slowly.

The S-42 had, however, a promised speed of 150mph (240kmh) which would carry its full payload of 32 passengers faster than its predecessor over the same routes, giving shorter journey times and improving the airline's schedules to further please the ever-increasing number of passengers. With a full payload of 32 passengers, the S-42 would have a non-stop range of 750 miles (1200km) – more than adequate for the non-stop trans-Caribbean route to Colombia – and permitted the omission of several *en route* points on the long route to Brazil and Argentina, where the S-40s and Commodores had to refuel.

A SIMPLE DESIGN

The S-42 would be a true flying-boat, powered by four Pratt & Whitney Hornet engines each developing 700hp. Gross weight would be just under 20 tonnes at take-off, or 39,000lb (17,700kg). In appearance, the S-42 was the most elegant flying-boat yet built, with a single one-piece wing of 114ft (34.7m) span. This wing carried the four Hornet radial engines, which faired into the leading edge and were tapered into place with metal cowlings. Below this wing, on either side, twin floats were

the S-42 been a landplane, concrete runways would have been needed to support the wheel loads, something then unheard of.

The four Hornet engines turned three-bladed propellers while the extra large wing flaps provided great lift for take-off and a strong braking action for landing, enabling the S-42 to land on the water at the same speed as the S-40. The three-bladed propellers were fitted with a variable pitch system which meant that the pilot could vary the propeller blade angle in flight according to speeds and conditions to provide for much greater efficiency. This new feature reduced fuel consumption thereby contributing to the aircraft's greater range.

With this design, the twin tail booms of the earlier Sikorskys were eliminated as were most of the struts and bracing wires. In overall appearance the S-42 was an elegant flying-boat.

LUXURY AND COMFORT

Fully equipped, including engines, propellers, instruments and radio, an S-42 would cost Trippe $242,000 a copy, but Trippe liked what he saw and placed an order with Sikorsky on 1 October 1932 for ten aircraft. The first of these was scheduled for delivery in mid-1934 and in the meantime Pan Am's interior design department (which comprised Trippe, a couple of planners and Charles Lindbergh) went to work. Progressively specifying their requirements to Sikorsky as the machine took shape, the group would make the S-42 the most elegantly appointed airliner yet, and airline publicists could use the word luxury for the first time and with confidence to describe the S-42's comfort standards.

While some arrangements provided for up to 38 passengers, standard seating on the S-42 was for 32, and these passengers sat in four compartments with eight seats in each. The seats were upholstered, had adjustable headrests and were positioned on each side of the spacious central aisle, carpeted in dark green. There were curtains at the windows and doorways separated six watertight compartments, any two of which could provide emergency buoyancy if necessary. The cabin walls were fitted with veneer panels in turquoise. Life jackets were carried under the floor, while the tail section contained a life-raft, flares, signal flags, sails, oars and water kegs. There were two toilets at the end of the cabin.

Sikorsky himself said of the S-42 that it represented simplicity in both its outline and its operational management. The aircraft had been designed for smooth and easy turn-arounds while giving passengers a high standard of comfort. All installations for control cables, fuel pipes etc. had been made suitable for easy inspection and maintenance. Eight elliptical fuel tanks with a total capacity of 1240 gallons (5636 litres) and four similar-shaped oil tanks of 74 gallons (336 litres) were cradled between the spars and compression chambers. Removable panels both above and below the wing afforded easy access for inspection and servicing. The refuelling system was designed specifically to save time in refuelling. The single intake pipe directed fuel under pressure to any one or all of the tanks by means of a series of control valves. On the flight deck (or cockpit as it was still known) special provision had been made to allow all instruments and their parts to be readily removed for checking and servicing.

The front baggage compartment of 157ft³ (4.4m³) was reached from the outside by a large hatch which could also enable passengers to exit in the event of an emergency. Two life-rafts were also stored here while a strong box for valuables was located under the floor. Additional baggage compartments were located at the rear of the aircraft near the main passenger stairway. In the passenger area the height overall was 6ft (1.8m) and the tubular construction of the seats was such that it eliminated seat legs, thus permitting an unobstructed space beneath each seat for luggage.

In the S-42 sound and vibration were given careful study and thick pads of sound-proofing materials were fitted in spaces behind the walls and ceiling of the aircraft. To eliminate vibration, springs in cushions were replaced by a special material.

Windows were held in place by rubber rings and without the need of fasteners that could cause shattering. In any passenger cabin, conversation could be carried on in a normal tone. A concealed ventilating system supplied upwards of 30ft³ (0.85m³) of air per passenger per minute. Auxiliary to this was an efficient exhaust system. Each cabin was equipped with safety belts and life belts. For inspection purposes, Sikorsky provided a walkway extending from bow to stern, and this walkway, together with ring walkways and engine platforms, made it possible to conduct almost any inspection or servicing operation without the need of an outside scaffold.

S-42 IN SERVICE

The first S-42 was completed in December 1933 and, because of bad weather, flight testing was postponed until the spring of 1934. The aircraft was taxied down the river from Sikorsky's factory and out into Long Island Sound. A series of test flights were begun by Captain Sergievsky in April 1934 and Pan American's chief pilot Captain Edwin Musick took over the flight test programme at Bridgeport in the summer of 1934. By 1 August 1934 the first S-42 was ready for its final flight tests, and together with Charles Lindbergh as his co-pilot, Musick began these test flights which were to establish a number of world records.

On completion of this programme the aircraft was flown to Miami, and on 16 August 1934 scheduled services from Miami to Rio de Janeiro began. The first commercial flight of the S-42 carried 19 passengers and a crew of eight. It visited 12 countries and colonies. On arrival in Rio de Janeiro the aircraft was christened *Brazilian Clipper* by the wife of the President of Brazil, Senora Vargas.

As the S-42 fleet was steadily delivered – through 1934, 1935, 1936 and 1937 – Pan American accumulated millions of miles of experience. Just as the Key West–Havana route had been a preliminary to expansion into the Caribbean and initial points in South America, this great continent now became a new point of departure for even longer range flights. In the period up until 1934 and the introduction of the S-42s, Pan American and its subsidiaries flew 11 million revenue aircraft miles (17.7 million km) with no fatal accidents. By 1934, Pan American operated some 54.5 per cent of the South American air route mileage, and taking Latin America as a whole, carried over 80 per cent of the traffic. By the end of 1934, aircraft fleet strength stood at 133 and the annual total passengers carried now numbered 160,875, the first time this total had reached six figures. Mail, the very life blood of the Pan Am services from the beginning, was now being carried at the rate of 2,000,000lb (900,000kg) a year, or 1000 tonnes. The Pan American route network now stretched for 31,250 miles (50,000km).

The Martin M-130, here shown in final assembly outside the Glenn L. Martin works at Baltimore in 1935.

CHAPTER SIX

Slow Boats to China

For Juan Trippe it was clear that flying-boats would continue to dominate the long-range network for some years to come because of the over-water or coastal nature of most routes. Pan American Airways was a long-range international airline and this meant the employment of long-range flying-boats. Even as he had awarded a contract to Sikorsky for his S-42 in 1932, Trippe contracted with aircraft manufacturer Glenn Martin to build him three Martin M-130 flying-boats, for Trippe was convinced he would need them to boost his fleet.

Such aircraft needed supporting, and Trippe was becoming ever more aware of the growing need for all the paraphernalia required to handle and maintain the aircraft while at their terminus and to process and embark passengers at each terminal point. Motor launches and maintenance hangars had to be built for the aircraft and rudimentary air terminals, with seats, coffee bars and ticket desks, had to be provided for passengers.

Increasing sums of money would be spent by Pan American on these facilities, but these were included among the capital assets by the accountants because a knock-on effect was seen when smart new passenger facilities replaced wooden huts and passengers grew in greater numbers to experience the attractions of this exciting new transport experience.

Thus, in 1933, construction work began on a magnificent new Pan American marine aircraft base at Coconut Grove, just south of Miami. The cost would be over $1 million but it would feature a fully equipped passenger terminal, docks, beaching facilities and hangars for the largest trans-ocean flying-boats and provision for passengers' automobiles. In Biscayne Bay a series of canals were dredged to serve as take-off lanes. This would be Pan American's main operating base from Miami and for the rest of the flying-boat era. It was known as the Dinner Key base and it came into full use in August 1934, replacing an earlier floating terminal at the same site. In December 1934 the second S-42 was delivered and this aircraft, named *West Indies Clipper* was used in Latin America. This aircraft was to be re-named *Pan American Clipper* and modified and used for Pacific survey flights. It suffered the indignity of a further name change in 1937 when it was re-christened *Hong Kong Clipper*.

While 4201, as it was numbered by the manufacturers, was given a profusion of names, 4202, the third aircraft, was delivered in May 1935 to Pan American but sadly never named at all – it was destroyed in an accident in Port of Spain, Trinidad, in December 1935.

Two more S-42s, the *Jamaica Clipper* and *Antilles Clipper,* were delivered in 1935 and a further two, *Brazilian Clipper* and *Dominican Clipper,* were delivered in 1936. All of these

aircraft were S-42 variants known as the S-42A; the original and initial S-42 was re-named the *Colombia Clipper* in 1937, thus accounting for the apparent duplication in the name of the sixth aircraft to be delivered. Two more variants were delivered over 1936 and 1937, these also being variants of the original model and known as the S-42B. They had a somewhat larger span – 118ft (36m) – and were a heavier model with a gross weight of 42,000lb (19,000kg). The model was even faster, with a maximum speed of 188mph (302kmh) and a cruising speed of 163mph (262kmh).

Of this total, six would be lost or destroyed (one by Japanese bombing), but during their period of operation the S-42 fleet carried thousands of passengers on the Latin America and Caribbean routes, up to the year 1946, serving well and honourably. *Colombia Clipper,* curiously, lasted longest. The first of the fleet to be delivered, in June 1934, this aircraft was finally scrapped in July 1946.

CONQUERING THE PACIFIC

In 1934, as the S-42s were coming off the production line and Glenn Martin was beginning serious work on the M-130, Trippe looked once again at the Pacific as a region that he was sure Pan American ought to be serving with flights to China

BELOW *The elegant M-130. In line with the practice of the day, dollies were used to move the aircraft to the water ready for operation.*

The M-130, seen here at Pan American's Dinner Key terminal, Miami, which was built specially by Pan American for its flying-boat operations.

and elsewhere. It was by no means clear that the S-42 was the right aeroplane for carrying on scheduled services across the Pacific, but this had to be tried and Captain Ed Musick shortly took off from Biscayne Bay and headed across the Gulf of Mexico on a route-proving flight to California. Musick flew the aircraft on to San Diego Naval Air Station for refuelling and provisioning. The aircraft then flew to San Francisco for an official send-off.

It was Musick's intention to fly to Honolulu and confront all the problems that might show themselves. Musick, Trippe and others had no illusions that there might be many problems. Little was known about Pacific weather, certainly where it concerned aeroplanes. Radio communication links were still rudimentary and there were, at the time, no suitable alternate bases at which to land should conditions require the aircraft to do so. In all of these areas, Pan American Airways was breaking new ground, and the pioneering work the airline conducted over these years would benefit many airline operators in the years to come. Constant performance records were kept during the flight and many new charts and graphs were devised to aid future operations.

The Pan American Clipper left San Francisco on 16 April 1935, and flying through the night the S-42 reached the Hawaiian Islands in the early hours of the following morning. The 2080 nautical miles (3350km) flight had taken 18 hours.

The return flight to San Francisco was made on 23 April and the newspapers reported triumphantly that the Pacific had been conquered. More survey flights were carried on over the next five months. Pan American carried out upper air soundings with the aid of red hydrogen balloons and weather maps were devised giving detailed wind patterns and forecasts. These survey flights were continued, until on 24 October 1935 Pan American was awarded a US Post Office contract for the carriage of trans-Pacific mail at the maximum rate of $2 per aircraft mile.

With the initial flights by the S-42s proving successful, the Pacific could hardly be said to have been conquered, especially as Trippe's intention was to extend the route to Manila in the Philippines. Intermediary bases were required, where the aircraft could put down on the water, taxi to tranquil inlets and be refuelled and serviced. As it happened, a number of such places were available, and these were to make a remarkable contribution to Pan Am's ultimate conquest of the Pacific.

With Hong Kong as a hoped-for ultimate terminal point off the coast of mainland China, stepping stones were required across this vast ocean area, which stretched from San Francisco to cover 8046 miles (12,960km) in total. It was typical of the good fortune that accompanied Trippe's endeavours that three islands were available at convenient intervals between San Francisco and Manila. From Honolulu, 1300 miles (2100km) to the northwest, was Midway Island, which had a cable company's radio station as its main occupant. This was US territory. Another 1200 miles (1930km) further west was the tiny Wake Island, believed at that point to be a coral atoll but in fact comprising three pinpoint islands in a group and enclosing a lagoon. Wake Island was not inhabited, and it was not even certain initially that it was in fact US territory. Finally, another 1560 miles (2500km)

to the west again was the considerably larger island of Guam, the most southerly of the Mariana Islands and which was inhabited by some 15,000 people. This again was US territory and would serve as a useful staging post to Manila, 1412 nautical miles (2270km) away. US Government approval was required before Pan American could establish bases on these islands, but this was not difficult to secure, for as the bases would be built largely at Pan American's expense, the US Navy saw these as valuable facilities in the event of some military emergency, while they could be seen as logical bases for extending the new and developing medium of air transport.

NORTH HAVEN LEADS THE WAY

Trippe had already applied to the US government for permission to establish air bases on the islands as far back as October 1934 and this was granted by March 1935; he also gained permission to operate a marine terminal in the Philippines a year later. Pan American had by now established a Pacific Division with its headquarters based at Alameda in

ABOVE *The Oakland Bay Bridge was another in the bridge-building programme of the 1930s. The 40-seat M-130 is pictured here as it passes over that bridge.*

BELOW *Interior seating arrangement on the M-130. Up to as many as 52 passengers could be carried on short flights.*

San Francisco Bay. Trippe now chartered a 15,000-tonne cargo ship, the *North Haven,* as the means by which he would build his air bases. *North Haven* left Pier 22 at San Francisco on 27 March 1935 with a remarkable load, including 250,000 US gallons (947,500 litres) of fuel, 44 airline technicians, 74 construction staff and the equivalent of two complete air bases. There were ten-tonne tractors, radio cars, launches, diesel engines, electric generators, prefabricated plywood buildings, water storage tanks and a large consignment of food. The beach at Sand Island, Midway, became a small tent village as materials were carried ashore by launch from the *North Haven,* which rode at anchor in the waters off Midway Island.

When a satisfactory base had been constructed at Midway, the working party and the *North Haven* sailed on to Wake Island, which was even more remote and practically a virgin island in the Pacific. While the *North Haven* had to lie off of Midway Island because of dangerous coral reefs, the lagoon at Wake Island was deep and therefore gave no problems. Supplies similarly had to be landed on Wake and hauled across the island for a base to be constructed. At Guam, construction work was straightforward as there had been a US naval base on the island

BELOW *An inspection party circa 1935 view the improvements in docking arrangements for the M-130 China Clipper. Note the large square windows, as opposed to the S-42's round ones.*

since 1917. A derelict navy facility was taken over to become Pan American's base of operations on the island. Guam was the easiest of the islands to convert to Pan American's needs, for the place had been used by flying-boats of the US Marines, and the hangars, workshops and store rooms that remained were reconstructed and adapted for use. The *North Haven* then continued on to Manila in the Philippines, mainly to collect further material for the Wake and Midway bases. By the time the ship reached Wake on the return journey, on 3 July, the aircraft dock had been completed, a solar water heating system constructed, and crew quarters built to provide a separate room for each crew member. There were hot showers, a storeroom, a powerhouse, two windmills and a pump house. At Midway there was an aircraft dock projecting 300ft (90m) from the beach into the sea, which was necessary to provide the 5-ft (1.5-m) draft required for the Pan American flying-boats. The *North Haven* finally returned to San Francisco on 28 July, just four months after leaving and with the bases for a trans-Pacific air route now reaching completion.

The construction of these air bases in so short a period of time was yet another of the remarkable feats that Pan American entered into in the pursuit of developing international air routes. Trippe had no idea when he began his first services that he would be called upon to provide bases for his aircraft and personnel, and with little interest in the construction of airports

ABOVE *The changeover to metal construction from wood is evident in this picture of the M-130 refuelling at the island of Guam. The sponsons had a variety of uses.*

he had entered into this task cheerfully and as a ready response to the need. He was now engaging personnel to construct fully-fitted air bases complete with piers and passenger terminals.

At Midway Island, the cable station on one side of the island was manned by 23 men, while Pan American's base on the other side, had a complement of 14. These apparently lonely outposts in the ocean had their attractions. 'All the comforts of home' were enjoyed by the men, who swam about in the warm clear waters when off-duty. Fish swam all around them and the bottom of the lagoons could be seen for 30ft (9m) out from the shore. A walk across the magnificent sandy beaches was a walk through scores of seabirds, including albatross, who were all quite unconcerned about the presence of men as they had no reason to fear them.

Enter Glenn Martin

When the S-42 was conceived for trans-ocean flying, the aircraft did not have anything approaching an economical payload–range performance for operations on the Pacific stages. The type was applied to the Caribbean network primarily, and while later the S-42 operated on the Manila–Hong Kong and also New York–Bermuda services, it was to give way to another type on the Pacific service, the Martin M-130.

Trippe had ordered three Martin M-130s at the same time as his initial order for the S-42 fleet back in 1932. When, in October 1935, Pan American took delivery of the first of the M-130s the S-42s were reassigned. While the initial route-proving and survey-flying had been done by the S-42s, the M-130s would be the types that now gained the glory for Pan Am's Pacific service. On 22 November 1935, the M-130s started the first revenue air service across the Pacific, just one month after Pan Am had been awarded the US foreign mail contract (the FAM 14) on 24 October 1935. Carrying mail and cargo only, and with Captain Ed Musick in command, the M-13O *China Clipper* headed westbound out of San Francisco Bay on the afternoon of 22 November to the cheers of a crowd of 125,000. On board with the seven-man crew were 110,865 letters.

The following day, the *China Clipper* covered the 2400 statute miles (3860km) to Honolulu at a cruising altitude of 10,000ft (3000m). At Honolulu an additional 4000lb (1800kg) was taken on for Wake and Guam in time for an early departure the following morning. Five days later, after a transit wait at Guam, the M-130 reached Manila on 29 November. The whole trip had involved 59 hours and 48 minutes of flying time. This inaugural service was the first ocean crossing by the *China Clipper* or indeed by any M-130.

The Martin M-130 was an aircraft different again to the Sikorsky S-42. This was Glenn Martin's biggest aircraft so far and its capacity and range was far greater than the S-42. Trippe had liked Martin's design when the drawings were first shown to him, in the same manner that he had warmed to the appearance of the S-42. He was nothing if not encouraging to the aircraft designers of the time who paid the right kind of attention to his needs.

Martin had been one of the earliest successful American aircraft designers and manufacturers, and by the time Trippe suggested he might take a look at his specification for a new flying-boat, he had 15 years' experience behind him. The US Army had bought six of his model-S seaplanes as far back as 1915, and the US Navy had bought one also. The little S float-plane was a biplane, and was followed by another seaplane in September 1916. Then came the Martin MB-1 a landplane bomber, which was used by US Marines to drop torpedoes and carry paratroops, who were perched precariously on the wings

RIGHT *Glenn L. Martin founded his aircraft company in 1912 and went on to supply the US military services. He was approached by Juan Trippe for a design in 1931 and produced the M-130.*

until the time of their mission. Several water-based aircraft followed for the military services, but none of these was particularly successful.

Then came the M-130, which would be a great technical success but which could have ruined Martin financially had it not been for World War II and his new and on-going success once again for the US Services. Martin worked best with the military, and he would later build successful World War II bombers, attack aircraft and flying-boats such as the *Marauder*, *Mauler*, *Mercator* and the *Mars* flying-boat.

Brought up in Kansas, Martin moved to Baltimore in 1928, where he bought a large piece of land to establish his new factory. The following years were financially disastrous for millions across the United States, and it appeared contrary to logic that anyone should want or be able to afford expensive aeroplanes when the United States was trying desperately to feed its citizens. But Trippe was a contradiction, and when he gave Martin an order for three M-130s he was unwittingly providing employment for a band of enthusiastic men and women, that would ultimately become a human tide in the most advanced industry in the world.

The M-130 Flying-boat

The M-130 flying-boat was a beautiful craft, seating up to as many as 52 passengers, with a cruising speed of 130mph (209kmh) and a total range capability of 3200 statute miles (5150km). It had a length of 91ft (27.7m) and a gross take-off weight of 26 tonnes, or 52,250lb (23,512kg). The long, boat-like hull was surmounted by a heavy single wing into which the engines were faired in the familiar manner and stabilising sponsons were fitted on either side of the lower fuselage, at water level, and were joined to the wing by the usual braces. While the M-130 was made mostly of aluminium alloy, the wing area aft of the rear spar was fabric covered. A notable

ABOVE *This picture reflects the comfortable atmosphere (for some) of the Pan Am flying-boat period. Note the carefree wave from the passenger in the launch and the photographer's camera.*

difference between that and Sikorsky's flying-boats was the single fin and rudder, which was tapered out of the elegant 90-ft (27-m) long rear fuselage. The wing area was 2145ft² (199m²) which excluded the 'seawings' (sponsons) whose area was 170ft² (15.7m²). The M-130's fuel capacity was 4000 US gallons (15,160 litres), or some 12 tonnes. The service ceiling was 17,000ft (5180m).

Even the comfort of the S-42 fleet was to be surpassed in Martin's M-130. The interior cabin was divided into eight compartments, the largest of which was a 16-ft (4.8-m) long lounge. There was provision for baggage in a forward compartment, a pair of toilets located on the starboard side and a further baggage compartment at the rear. As the M-130 was intended for long, over-water flights of considerable duration, bunks could be converted from the settee-type seating pairs, where passengers would have their first experience of sleeping overnight in the air. There was a galley equipped with a refrigerator, sink and grill for preparing hot meals. The eight-man crew – comprising a captain, two flying officers, junior pilot, flight engineer and his assistant, a radio operator and steward – had provision for rest, two at a time, in a pair of bunks in the rear of the aircraft.

Up to 52 passengers could be carried on very short flights, but on a normal service there was a maximum capacity for 46. In the first months of the Pacific service mail only would be carried. When complete trans-Pacific services were introduced, in October 1936, the passenger payload was reduced to well below 40 for the entire journey and in some cases this was reduced to no more than 16 passengers and sometimes well below that, simply because of the absolute necessity of carrying enough fuel for the critical California–Hawaii segment.

For the San Francisco–Honolulu leg, the fuel load, including reserves for emergencies, had to be so substantial as to preclude more than a few passengers. For other stages fuel requirements were not so critical and would-be travellers were ready to pay the $799 one-way fare from San Francisco to Manila, or $360 for the shorter trip to Hawaii. The standard baggage allowance at the time was 55lb (25kg) per passenger. Passengers were ready to be pampered by stewards serving the best quality food from the finest bone china, set on spotless linen tablecloths and using sterling silver tableware. For those travelling on the through route to Manila, a maximum of 18 sleeping berths were available. The actual flight time was some sixty hours, but for business executives and others the air service reduced the travel time to six days compared with the several weeks required by ocean liners.

WORLD DOMINATION

With the M-130, Pan American Airways became the world's dominant trans-oceanic airline. The publicity was immense and Trippe had become rightly famous as a successful airline entrepreneur. Pan American services in other regions such as South America and the Caribbean continued to do well and other aircraft, such as DC-2 landplanes were introduced by Panagra for its west South American routes, which brought Buenos Aires within five-and-a-half days of the United States. Heavy investments were still being made on behalf of Pacific Alaska Airways, both for the development of new routes and for the acquisition of new aircraft able to operate more reliably under the harsh Alaskan conditions. Two Lockheed L-10 Electras were acquired for Pacific Alaska in 1934, and these were fitted by the airline with skis and other special equipment for freezing conditions.

One interesting new type to be developed especially for Pan American was another Sikorsky type, the S-43. This was a twin-engined 'baby clipper' amphibian for the coastal and other routes in the Caribbean. The S-43 was introduced in 1936 to replace the now ageing Commodores which had served Pan American well and probably even better than had been expected. The S-43s carried up to 18 passengers and were later to operate in Brazil and for a short time on the west South American coast. A variant, which had no wheeled undercarriage, was designated the S-43B. Thirteen S-43s and variants were ordered by Pan American for Panagra and Panair do Brasil but only four were operated by Pan Am. None of them were ever named.

Most of the S-38s, Fokker VIIs and Commodores were now phased out and replaced by new and better aircraft. Most of the S-40s continued in service for another two or three years. All flying was still done in daylight hours only, but Pan Am's excellent standards of service ensured that the traffic figures remained high, and while the airline was still heavily dependent upon mail revenue for income, passenger traffic was now making a marked impression.

THE M-130 IN SERVICE

The first Martin M-130 was handed over to Pan American on 9 October 1935 at Martin's Baltimore plant in Middle River, and was accepted by Trippe and Lindbergh, who was accompanying him. The aircraft began its mail services on 22 November, under the command of Captain Ed Musick and this aircraft began a momentous new service. While the elegant flying-boat was the best that had been seen yet, it had operational limitations which were to limit the true commercially viable air services that Trippe had in mind. Time and technology were still major issues, and Trippe always seemed to be trying to shorten one and advance rapidly on the other. He gave his passengers the best kind of service that was possible but he knew in his heart that things could be and would be a lot better in due course.

In the spring of 1936, cargo was being carried across the Pacific as well as mail, and this regular payload was increasing in volume. Preparations had to be made for the passenger services on the Pacific route and in the period before their commencement the time was put to good use. At the bases of Midway, Wake and Guam attractive single-storey hotels were built and set among lawns and tastefully designed gardens. Each hotel contained 24 double bedrooms fitted with shower baths and a permanent staff to provide the highest standards of service and catering.

Once again Pan American chartered the *North Haven*, this time loaded with furniture, pillows, solar water heaters and great quantities of equipment for these three passenger transit stations. The once barren island outposts were transformed into luxurious transit stops. In the summer of 1936, the M-130s were given a complete interior renovation and fitted out as flying hotels in readiness for the Pacific passenger services.

NEGOTIATING THE WAY

On 14 November 1935 a second M-130, named *Philippine Clipper* had been delivered and joined the *China Clipper* mail/cargo service. After complex and tediously long negotiations with the Chinese, including purchase by Pan American of a share in the Chinese airline CNAC, rights had been gained to operate a mail service between Shanghai and Canton in 1933. This operation, historic in itself, gave Pan American a further link in the chain. Then, in 1936, landing rights in the British Crown colony of Hong Kong were granted, and the *Philippine Clipper* had the distinction of making a special flight from Manila to Hong Kong to mark the occasion. While he was unable to serve the route in the manner that he intended, Trippe could at least now say that Pan American Airways operated scheduled services across the Pacific Ocean.

The flights between San Francisco and down to Manila were operated at a frequency of once weekly in 1936 and up to the

point when the first scheduled passenger flights were begun, in October 1936. This was to be a truly memorable date for Pan American Airways, and hard-earned, for the bargaining for route rights that was required before these services could be operated often took more time than the development and introduction into service of a new aeroplane, involving Pan American and US State officials, various foreign diplomats and the governments of other countries.

In 1931, the Japanese occupied China on a pretext and in 1932 Japanese troops invaded it. Tensions grew in the Pacific, and by 1936 the Japanese were formally complaining to the US government that the island bases at Midway, Wake and Guam were actually being developed for military purposes rather than the purely innocent purposes for Pan American. As US flying-boats could now reach China, military implications were imagined by the Japanese.

Such arguments were rejected and dismissed by the US government and Pan American flew on. Honour for the operation of the first scheduled passenger service went to the M-130 *Hawaiian Clipper,* which embarked on the flight to Honolulu on 21 October 1936. This first passenger flight carried nine passengers and was a great success. Each M-130 had cost Pan American $417,000 fully equipped, but Trippe felt the cost was worth it.

The contract to build the three aircraft had been the subject of hard negotiation between Trippe and Martin. Pointing out that the largest contemporary landplane then in operation, the Douglas DC-2, cost just $78,000 a copy, Trippe rejected outright Martin's proposal to build and equip

the three aircraft for just under $2 million in total. Martin might have broken even on a unit price of $500,000, but Trippe, ever the hard bargainer, argued for less. Martin, fully aware that he needed the work and the money, finally agreed to a price of $417,000 each.

While Trippe was satisfied, Martin was stoical. With all aircraft complete and all equipment and spares supplied, he was out of pocket on the deal. However, he was in discussions with the US Navy and he was hopeful that Trippe might ask for additional, developed versions of the M-130 to amplify the Pacific fleet. In the event, Trippe never bought another M-130, although he looked seriously at Martin's proposed follow-on type, the M-157. Two years after delivery of the last M-130 Clipper to Pan American, however, the navy ordered the Martin XPB2M-1 *Mars,* the US Navy's largest flying-boat. The wing span of this aircraft was 200ft (61m) and the gross weight 72.5 tonnes, or 145,000lb (65,250kg). The M-130s wearing Pan American colours flew across the Pacific for the next nine years. The Martin company's financial position was secured and on-going work was guaranteed.

The M-130s operated steadily on the service from October 1936, with a once-weekly schedule between San Francisco and Manila, in a round trip elapsed time of 13 days, which included a two-day stop at Manila. With increased experience, and as the initial teething troubles on the first trans-Pacific flights were

RIGHT *The cockpit compartment of the M-130. Note
the spartan crew seats.*

BELOW *Arrival of an M-130
in the Pacific, illustrating
the great number of craft
required to support the
airliner, which would have
ranged from refuelling tank-
ers to catering craft, engine
servicing vehicles and vessels
carrying cleaners.*

for none reached honourable retirement.

In November 1936 the Shanghai–Canton service was extended to Hong Kong to complete the Chinese link, and mail contracts were obtained for operation from the Portuguese colony of Macao, effective from 28 April 1937. Additionally, rights were gained for operation of services to New Zealand, although these were to be short-lived.

Pan American Airways Clipper flying-boats were now known the world over and identified by schoolboys and

eliminated, it was possible to reschedule the flights to enable an entire round trip from San Francisco to Hong Kong and back to be completed by the M-130 in 14 days. With the award of an operating permit from what was then the British Crown Colony of Hong Kong on 17 September 1936, an S-42B was delivered to the Pacific Division for the purpose of flying once a week between Manila and Hong Kong, to connect with the Martin M-130 service which then terminated at Manila. With the refinement of the M-130 schedules, the S-42B operation was no longer required and was withdrawn. In later years the triumphant trio of M-130s would be said to have been ill-fated

everyone interested in aviation and the airlines. Publicity films were made and passengers waxed lyrical about the superlative comforts of this wonderful medium of travel. Hollywood even made a film starring Humphrey Bogart about the services, *China Clipper*. At the end of 1936, 141 aircraft were flying in the colours of Pan American Airways or its affiliated companies, such as Panagra, Panair do Brasil and Pacific Alaska Airways, on routes stretching halfway across the world. Passengers carried during the year totalled 166,468 and total revenue for the year was sum $10,400,000, which yielded a profit of $55,350. Pan Am and its subsidiaries now employed a workforce of 4108.

The majesty of flight. An M-130 is pictured here as it cruises off the coast of California.

CHAPTER SEVEN

Travail and Tragedy

The year 1938 started badly for Pan American and would continue that way. Trippe was already aware that the trans-Pacific route was losing money despite its apparent success (1100 applications had been received for the seven places available to fare-paying passengers on the inaugural flight) and he was looking forward to the introduction of even better aircraft to change the situation.

Trippe was aware that in the period before the arrival of the new aircraft (and that would not be until January 1939), something had to be done to make the route viable. The maintenance required to enable the aircraft to carry on the scheduled services, coupled with the high expense of the air bases on the remote islands, produced a heavy drain on resources, and the income from mail and passengers was not matching the expenses. While they were fine aircraft, the Martin M-130s just did not have the payload-range capability to make them profit-earners, particularly over the critical 2400-mile (3800-km) long stretch from San Francisco to Honolulu.

While Trippe was pondering the problem, the first catastrophe occurred on the routes which dealt a severe blow – Pan American lost an aircraft and its crew and Trippe lost a friend. On the same day that Pan American opened the trans-Pacific mail service, on 22 November 1935, an agreement had been signed with the New Zealand government for landing rights at Auckland. By the time Pan Am was ready to operate the New Zealand service, between Honolulu and Auckland, however, the Martin M-130s were fully occupied on the route to the Orient. Pan American decided instead to begin the service to New Zealand with the S-42B. The first flight took place on 23 December 1937, and a successful return flight was made by way of Kingman Reef, a dot of land 1100 miles (1770km) southwest of Honolulu.

ABOVE *Although the M-130 could carry up to 46 passengers, sometimes capacity was reduced to only five or six passengers because of the critical fuel requirements on long stages.*

BELOW *Pan American acquired two smaller Sikorsky amphibians for use by subsidiary companies, the S-41 and the S-43 (shown here). Both were powered by Pratt & Whitney Hornet engines.*

On its second scheduled flight, however, on 11 January 1938, Captain Ed Musick was at the tiny island of Pago Pago in Samoa, one of the islands selected as a refuelling point for the service, when disaster struck. While these beautiful island locations in the South Pacific were useful for such stops, most of them had limitations and Pago Pago was no exception. With the S-42B fully fuelled, Musick took off for the final leg to Auckland. Some way out over the Pacific the aircraft developed engine trouble and Musick decided to return. The aircraft never reached Pago Pago, fishermen reporting later that the S-42B *Samoan Clipper* had been seen to be on fire. Shortly after it had crashed into the sea. Musick and his crew of six men were all lost in this first crash of a Pan American Clipper on the over-water services. The accident report showed that fuel vapours had been ignited by the hot engines in the act of jettisoning fuel and this caused an explosion. As a result of this, Pago Pago was withdrawn as a refuelling point and the New Zealand service temporarily suspended. This was the first of the troubles that befell Pan American and Trippe in 1938.

FRIENDS IN HIGH PLACES

There was some relief for Trippe, however, for the value of his airline was soon to be recognised in high places. President Franklin D. Roosevelt had entered office in 1933, having resoundingly defeated President Hoover in 1932, and in February 1934 Roosevelt cancelled all domestic air-mail contracts in the face of charges of bribery and other corrupt activities, such as the formation of cartels. This did not affect Pan American directly but charges were laid against the airline on the grounds of favouritism shown in the granting of international air-mail contracts and traffic rights. A Post Office investigation was made in 1935, and showed that Pan American's mail contracts had been settled by negotiation, rather than by competitive bidding as required under US law. It was concluded, however, that the cancellation of the airline's mail contracts would be against the public interest, in both the United States and the foreign countries served. It was acknowledged that Pan American had started these services and deserved some credit for that fact. Equally, the airline could not readily be replaced.

The US Post Master James Farley invited airlines to tender for new contracts in 1935, and shortly this matter was settled. In 1938, with President Roosevelt firmly in power as the most respected president for many years, a new Civil Aeronautics Act was introduced. With the passing of this Act, Trippe presented the case for a review of the air-mail rates paid to Pan American, which were still being paid at the rate of $2 per mile, the maximum which had been laid down under the Foreign Airmail Act of March 1929. The Civil Aeronautics Board heard the case

in February and March 1939, and to Trippe's delight issued an order increasing the mail rate to $3.35 per mile, effective from 1 April 1939.

This did not help Pan American in 1938, but with a new guaranteed income from mail it would be possible to improve the Pacific services and ensure continuing operation of the fleet, which would be further improved.

OVERCOMING PROBLEMS

The last S-42 had been delivered in 1937, and the M-130s were being worked hard on the Pacific routes. The M-130 had its problems and limitations as all aircraft do. The engines had a tendency to overheat, and the original 830-hp Pratt & Whitney Twin Wasps were replaced by four 900-hp versions, which were later uprated to 950hp. The engines were Pratt & Whitney's first production commercial R-1830 models. The propellers were Hamilton Standard constant speed types of the hydromatic kind, which meant that they could be braked in the event of an engine shut-down; at that point propeller feathering had not yet been developed.

Talking of his work on these engines in a lecture to the Royal Aeronautical Society in November 1980, Mr John G. Borger explained the problems. Borger worked for Pan American for 45 years, joining the airline in 1935 as an engineer and retiring in 1980 as vice-president and chief engineer. His paper covered the development of engines used over the period in the Pan American fleet, and of the M-130 he explained that the Pratt & Whitney 1830s were the first to have cowl flaps installed, presumably to permit greater cooling air flow during low-speed operations and to reduce cooling drag at cruising speeds. At the low cruising speeds necessary to obtain the best fuel consumption it was necessary to open the cowl flaps to maintain cylinder head temperatures within limits. The increased drag resulting from this reduced the forward speed. This required increased power, which in turn increased the temperatures of the cylinder heads and which necessitated opening of the cowl flaps again!

Borger said that the problem was finally brought under control by replacing the cowling side panels and flaps with flared flaps with a somewhat greater exit gap. The flared cowls were installed at the same time as the modified 950-hp engines with higher activity propellers and together these permitted the raising of the allowable gross weight from just over 26 tonnes, or about 52,000lb (23,400kg). At this point a typical overhaul life of proven aircraft engines in the Pan Am fleet was some 450 hours, which was sufficient for perhaps six months' flying at contemporary utilisation figures.

COMPETITION

Pan American Airways was by no means operating in a vacuum in this period as airliners, wearing the colours of all kinds of operators, were now flying on scheduled services to different parts of the world. Great Britain had reached the countries of its empire, taking in South Africa, Australia and India with passenger services backed by its Empire Air Mail scheme; France was flying to points throughout Continental Europe, North Africa and to Indo-China through the medium of its flag-carrier Air France; KLM Royal Dutch Airlines was performing similarly and to points in the Dutch East Indies; Germany's Luft Hansa, one of the best airlines in Europe, operated a network of services that took in numerous points in South America.

None of the aircraft used by these carriers were any better than those used by Pan American and most of them were poorer. In spite of their limited range on the Pacific services, the Martin M-130s were reliable, luxurious and business-like, with a soundness of construction and elegance that engendered confidence in their passengers, many of whom were flying for the first time. As fuel and mail had to constitute most of the

ABOVE *Tea is served. Details of this flight are unknown, but later Pan American was to settle on white jackets for the pursers rather than the attire shown here.*

loads carried on the long stages, passengers had to be given lower priority, and on the long leg between San Francisco and Honolulu no more than eight to ten passengers could be frequently carried. These passengers were consequently well provided for, and could stretch out in three large compartments and an even larger lounge/dining salon. With cocktails in the lounge, formal evening meals and Pullman bunks for the night, the China Clippers, as they came to be called, acquired a reputation for luxury which extended well beyond US and Pacific shores.

From San Francisco to Hawaii the journey took 18–20 hours, but it was such a wondrous experience that passengers were not deterred. For those who had the money the high fares were no deterrent either – the round-trip fare to Honolulu of $720, and $1600 round trip San Francisco–Manila fare, were paid by the rich, famous and those valuing the great time-savings involved.

No one talked about the discomforts of the flights, which would be totally unacceptable today. Pressurised cabins had not then been introduced, and so the flights were made at altitudes generally approximating 8000ft (2400m). Coupled with this was enduring the thundering noise of the engines that carried on for long hours. As the total flying time to Manila was sixty hours, spread over five days, passengers would have been glad of a rest at that point.

By 1935, Trippe had his eyes fixed firmly on the North Atlantic. His engineers prepared specifications for a new model to succeed the M-130 which would be able to do much more than that elegant craft ever could. Martin's flying-boat had performed well enough, and he responded readily to Pan American's invitation for a follow-on aircraft with a series of new models, which he hoped would ensure continuance of the Martin commercial flying-boat line. Designs were developed for Martin models numbered 152 to 157, and eventually the model 157 was submitted. This was a scaled up 57-seat version of the model 130, with a gross weight of 70,000lb (31,500kg) or approximately 35 tonnes. Martin still had development costs of $500,000 to deal with resulting from the loss he had made on the M-130s. Without a fresh order these would have

BELOW *The winged globe symbol featured only the South American continent and Caribbean for years before a style change was made to reflect the growing network.*

to be written off. A new order would not be forthcoming from Trippe, however, for a new entrant, Boeing, was to win this competition.

Everything had gone so smoothly for Trippe since he had first been able to prove Pan American Airways as a commercially viable airline, that experiencing insurmountable difficulties would be a totally new situation for him. Pan American had so far been a one-man crusade and he had run the airline almost as a personal fiefdom. Difficulties had plagued Trippe on many an occasion, but there had always been a willing and friendly investor amongst his wealthy associates who would simply write another cheque and the problem would be solved. Great sums of money were being spent by the airline. On the trans-Pacific service, however, the increasing cost of surface establishments and the airline infrastructure as a whole were running well ahead of what the airline could really afford.

THE MARTIN MYSTERY

In July 1938 came another disaster which would temporarily cripple Pan Am further and which would cast a shadow over the airline's shining image. As this disaster was a mystery that would never be solved, Pan Am's difficulties were to be compounded.

On 23 July, during routine operations in the Pacific, the three China Clippers were positioned at various destinations: the *China Clipper* was on its way back to Alameda Bay, San Francisco, from Hong Kong; the *Philippine Clipper* was in mid-Pacific *en route* for the Far East; the *Hawaii Clipper,* which had now made 35 Pacific round trips, was making what appeared to be another routine flight. It carried a full crew and 14 passengers and carried the usual emergency equipment, including a radio complete with trailing antenna, an auxiliary generator, rubber rafts, shotguns, fishing tackle, bait and provisions, all stored in an emergency locker. In addition, the aircraft had been re-fitted only two months earlier with upgraded, 950-hp Pratt & Whitney engines and the new hydromatic

propellers. Any two engines could keep the Clipper flying if there was engine trouble. The *Hawaii Clipper* had flown the first four legs of the flight, from San Francisco to Honolulu, to Midway, Wake and then to Guam without remark, and the

ABOVE *Havana–Nassau (Bahamas) publicity material of the period featured the S-42. Key West can be seen, from where flights began.*

LEFT *By July 1939, the Boeing 314 was being advertised by Pan American Airways System in timetables for the Atlantic services.*

aircraft then took off in the early morning of 28 July 1938 for the onward leg to Manila.

There was nothing to make this stage any different from the others as far as was known, and the radio operator sent a position report just after noon giving the aircraft's location as 12 degrees 27 minutes north latitude and 130 degrees 40 minutes east longitude. The ground speed was given as 112 knots, or 129mph (207kmh).

At 11 minutes after noon the radio operator on the island of Panay, the closest radio station to the Clipper's position, acknowledged the report, at which point communications ceased. As the *Hawaii Clipper* was not heard from again in spite of Panay's constant attempts, the radio station contacted all the Pacific bases asking for information, and then

ABOVE *Pan American bought a total of 12 S-43 'Baby Clippers' for its subsidiaries. The craft pictured here was destined for Panair do Brazil.*

requested their move to emergency standby. By the evening of 28 July the worst was feared and the US Navy was alerted to begin a sea search. The following day, and in the days that followed up to 5 August, the US Navy despatched ships and aircraft to methodically search a vast sea area, crossing and re-crossing the *Hawaii Clipper's* last reported position.

As the search area was widened, the mystery grew deeper, as not a trace of the aircraft could be found or anything relating to its presence in the area. No pieces of aircraft or wreckage of any kind, including debris, life-rafts or personal possessions from the passengers could be discovered. The *Hawaii Clipper* had simply disappeared without trace and was never heard of again.

The Pacific was an increasingly dangerous place at this time, with the Japanese becoming ever more bellicose, and as with the mysterious disappearance of the famous female American pilot Amelia Earhart during a Pacific flight in 1937, the Japanese occasioned a fair amount of suspicion in regard to the *Hawaii Clipper.* They were said to be constructing secret military bases on their own Pacific islands while they were pointedly accusing the United States in regard to its own. There was no proof whatsoever of any aggressive intent against the *Hawaii Clipper,* but more bewildering was the fact that no clue could be found over the period of the search or at any time thereafter to offer an explanation for the aircraft's disappearance. One report was made of a large circle of oil on the ocean's surface in the area of the last reported position, while another report said that no oil slick was ever seen.

The third and final M-130 to be delivered to Pan American, the loss of the *Hawaii Clipper* now reduced the fleet to two and

this would place great strain on the maintenance of the Pacific services. This was not the first time that the finger of suspicion had been pointed at the Japanese. On 5 January 1936, the first M-130 to be delivered, the *China Clipper,* was on the point of making an afternoon departure for Honolulu when the aircraft hit an obstruction in the water as it was taxiing to the take-off point, tearing its hull.

Upon investigation a large concrete block with iron rods encased in it was found to be lying in the waters of the bay, placed in a dangerous manner. Pan American and FBI investigators found no explanation for this obstruction, but it appeared to be a serious attempt at sabotage. In an earlier reported but unpublicised incident, two Japanese were interrupted in the act of mis-calibrating the radio direction finder of the *China Clipper* two days before a flight from the Alameda base, in 1935.

With the *Hawaii Clipper* missing, the S-42Bs had to be repositioned to augment the two other China Clippers wherever possible, and while the Pacific fleet of M-130s had never been enough, new and better aircraft to take over would not be delivered for another six months. Trippe was looking at a new flying-boat fleet as the vehicles for the trans-Atlantic service, which he had been planning for years. With the new fleet he would have to ensure that there were sufficient aircraft for all his needs, which is why he had ordered a first six.

TROUBLE FOR TRIPPE

Meanwhile, losses mounted and the new mail rates had not yet become a subject of discussion in the Civil Aeronautics Board. Trippe felt alone, and bereft even of the company and wisdom of his friend Charles Lindbergh, who had long gone, leaving Pan American and the United States in December 1935 in the wake of a personal tragedy. In March 1932, his baby son Charles had been kidnapped and a ransom demanded. In a personal effort to deal quickly with the matter and avoid an on-going tide of publicity Lindbergh paid. The baby was found dead, the suspected murderer caught and a trial held in 1935. Over this long period, however, the publicity became worse and the atmosphere fouled. Unable to take it any longer, Lindbergh and his distraught wife left the United States for England, for

what they hoped was a peaceful haven. They rented a house in Kent where they were mostly unknown, and after the convicted man had been executed back in the United States, they gradually recovered from their ordeal.

In the following years the Lindberghs toured European capitals, dined with the King of England, and inspected Goering's Luftwaffe at his invitation. It was not until April 1939 that the Lindberghs returned to America, to find Trippe, totally demoted in status, as a man who had almost lost his empire.

The troubles for Trippe had come to a head towards the end of 1938, when the company directors became aware of the seriousness of the financial situation and called Trippe to account. The airline was heavily in debt and the Pacific routes

ABOVE *The S-43 'Baby Clipper' was powered by two Pratt & Whitney Hornet engines and had the capacity to carry a total of 18 passengers. The S-43B version pictured here had twin tails.*

continued to lose money heavily in spite of their appeal to passengers. The loss of the *Hawaii Clipper* made the position worse, and while this was no fault of Trippe's, the airline had now lost two important aeroplanes. Most importantly, there would be no dividend for shareholders from the financial results at the end of the year and this would make an impression on a lot of important people who travelled with Pan Am.

Someone had to be accountable, and that person was Trippe. His imperious ways and profligate spending of other people's money were derided, and to his distress, he was removed as the executive head of the airline. Cornelius 'Sonny' Whitney, a majority shareholder, was made chief executive officer as well as chairman of the board. Trippe was in no position to complain, as his old friend had part-financed the airline from the beginning and had always been ready with further funds when they were needed. Now, he was the boss and Trippe had to accept the fact.

When the year's results were set down for the annual report, an operating profit of no more than $46,672 was recorded for 1938 and which was offset by heavy debts and massive financial liabilities. In March 1939, the board was realigned and Trippe retained the title of president, but this was now not much more than honorary. It was made clear that day-to-day decisions were no longer his responsibility.

Special docks had to be constructed by Pan Am on the Pacific islands, and these were used as staging posts for Clippers making the long journey across the ocean.

CHAPTER EIGHT

Bermuda Triangle

Fortunately for Trippe, his time in the wilderness would be relatively brief, and it was perhaps good for the world at large that the man who had been bent on an aviation career from the age of 12 would shortly be reinstated as the prime mover in Pan American.

Before his demotion, Trippe had pursued many lines of interest and he remained fascinated with the North Atlantic. In many ways he was a dreamer, which was no bad thing because some of man's finest schemes have come from a passionate belief in what is possible. As early as May 1919, Trippe had written in the Yale college magazine that 'flights across the Atlantic Ocean should be perfectly safe as a commercial proposition and not a gigantic gamble'. Less than twenty years later the groundwork had been done by Pan Am for such flights.

As early as 1929, Trippe had initiated a programme to investigate all possible air routes across the Atlantic and even at that date he had held preliminary conversations with representatives of Imperial Airways of England and of the Compagnie Générale Aéropostale of France with a view to collaboration. At that date bilateral air agreements were hardly the concern of governments, and Pan American Airways, which generally meant Juan Trippe, carried out negotiations over routes and landing rights directly with airline representatives.

Taking his famous ball of string, Trippe measured the distances and considered the best possible routes across the Atlantic. One of these was a northerly route, by way of Newfoundland, Greenland and Iceland, to perhaps Copenhagen or England. Charles Lindbergh had advocated the northern route in 1932 when Pan American sponsored a number of expeditions for the purpose of accumulating data for future trans-Atlantic operations. Most ambitious was Lindbergh's flight to Scandinavia by way of Greenland and Iceland in 1933. With

the aid of a supply ship, Lindbergh was able to assess the effects of *en route* conditions on aircraft, and examine possible airport sites and the operating problems of such a route. Lindbergh flew as far east as Moscow and returned by way of Portugal and the South Atlantic using his specially outfitted Lockheed Sirius.

Another possible route was that through the mid-Atlantic, using Bermuda and the Azores to Lisbon and up to Southampton or Marseilles. As Imperial Airways of Britain was already pursuing the idea of a trans-Atlantic service to expand its own network, certain horse-trading had to be done over route rights and landing places. In this regard Imperial Airways was strongly placed, for the airline was owned and operated by the state, Bermuda was a Crown Colony and the aircraft manufacturer Short Brothers was in the process of developing long-range flying-boats specifically for such a service.

Perhaps it was the excitement of the time, but to the surprise of many the Portuguese granted in the summer of 1930 exclusive landing rights to Compagnie Générale Aéropostale for the Azores–Lisbon sector. Imperial Airways and Pan American

decided it would be circumspect to form a joint operating company for trans-Atlantic services, and on 14 May 1930 the Pan American–Imperial Airways company was founded. Apart from the fact that no aircraft existed with range capability for Atlantic services in 1930, it was really all too early for such a move. In any case, Aéropostale's financial position was shaky and shortly the airline went out of business. An agreement permitting Pan American to use the former Aéropostale landing concession in the Azores was concluded on 1 January 1932, but a year later the licence was revoked through non-performance.

RACE FOR THE ATLANTIC

Much had to be done before the trans-Atlantic route could become the prize of Pan American, Imperial Airways or anyone else, and this meant development of the aircraft as well as the establishment of proper new bases. For Pan American in the 1930s priority had to be given to services already operating. The S-42s had never been designed for trans-Pacific services and these were now being used to support the Martin M-130

fleet. Larger and longer-range aircraft were required altogether and Trippe hoped that a manufacturer would come up with the aircraft that he needed for the task, perhaps to buy in quantity.

On 1 July 1930 there had been another exciting development with the granting of rights to operate a Bermuda–United States service by the Legislative Council of Bermuda. This permission lapsed in April 1932, however, and in due course Pan Am and Imperial would have to start again.

In 1935, Pan American recorded the fact with the US State Department that it wished to start a trans-Atlantic air service before long, and on 12 December 1935 the US State Department announced that it had reached agreement with several countries over the operation of such services. When Great Britain advised the US Secretary of Commerce that it would grant Pan American a permit for operation subject to the US government's approval of that airline, things took another step forward. Approval was given by the US government to Pan American in September 1936 and it appeared to be not too long now before the world would see some trans-Atlantic flights.

In furtherance of the objective of enacting flights across the ocean, Pan Am then pursued the Portuguese government to grant landing rights to the Azores which had lapsed with the demise of Aéropostale. While the airline did not necessarily want to fly to Lisbon, this route did at least provide a means of crossing the Atlantic; the Azores, a Portuguese-owned group of islands about 1000 miles (1600km) due west of Portugal, could serve as a very useful stopping point on the way to Europe. At the same time, the airline applied to the French government for a permit to operate to one or more points in France.

ABOVE *Pan American established bases on the Pacific Islands for overnight stops including Wake Island, here visited by an M-130.*

RIGHT *The S-42 type was used in both the Caribbean and Latin America and also went on to see service in the Pacific.*

LEFT *The passenger terminal was in the early stages of its development, but it had come a long way from the simple wooden building, and already carried illuminated signs.*

BELOW *In the early years, the best Pan Am could do was to fly a banner from the front of the passenger terminal.*

POLITICS AND PERMITS

The long delays incurred in the granting of permission to operate these routes led Pan American and Imperial Airways to take a fresh look at the northern route by way of Newfoundland, Greenland and Iceland. If this proved feasible, Pan Am proposed to begin services from the United States to Copenhagen, and this concept produced a measure of success in that Pan American obtained permission for the construction of a radio station in Iceland, which was established in 1936. Prospects looked rather better now in that there was promise, if long-term, for services across the Atlantic by one route or another, the north or the south, and activity was maintained on the matter of clearing the way for through services.

More delays were experienced in the granting of permits, however, this time by Newfoundland, where prospects had initially seemed very promising. Pondering another idea, in 1936 Pan Am considered a service between Reykjavik and Stavanger, Norway, to reach Europe by way of the Faroe Islands and Shetlands in collaboration with the Norwegian carrier Det Norske Luftfarteslskap (DNL). Following a firm agreement to this effect, DNL placed an order for one Sikorsky S-43, to be delivered two months later. The aircraft was delivered late, however, and as a result of technical difficulties this project was initially postponed and then abandoned.

After lengthy negotiations, Pan Am finally obtained rights from Great Britain to operate between the United States and London by the northern or southern routes in addition to operating services from New York to Bermuda and Newfoundland on a strictly reciprocal basis with Imperial Airways. This was in February 1937, and on 22 February the United Kingdom's Director General of Civil Aviation was able to authorise Pan Am to operate a civil air service into the UK for a service terminating at an airport serving London. The United States granted reciprocal rights to Imperial Airways and similar permits were obtained the same year from Canada, Bermuda and the Republic of Ireland.

Discussions with Portugal finally paid off likewise, and in 1937 landing rights were granted to Pan American for the Azores and Portugal. The airline had already entered into negotiations for flights to other European countries, including Spain and Germany.

Thus, in the spring of 1937, Pan Am established an Atlantic Division with a view to beginning operations on the New York–Bermuda route as soon as possible. Two S-42Bs were allocated to the division, the latter being modified for North Atlantic survey flights. After a series of trial and training flights, the inaugural Pan American service was made over the 750-mile (1200-km) stretch from Port Washington, New York, to Hamilton, Bermuda, on 18 June 1937, closely followed by Imperial Airways' operations. Under the agreement they had made, Pan American and Imperial Airways undertook handling and servicing tasks for each other's aircraft at New York and Bermuda. The initial service frequency was one round trip weekly per carrier, but this frequency was doubled after two months.

THE GOLDEN LINK

The Bermuda operation provided a boost service for both Pan American and Imperial Airways, and with landing rights and all necessary permits in hand, both airlines were able to make a start over this important link. The importance of Bermuda could not be underestimated. A British Crown Colony (now called an 'Overseas Territory') lying as a collection of dots in the Atlantic, 537 miles (917km) off the east coast of mainland America, Bermuda actually constituted 150 islands covering 21 miles^2 (54km^2). The capital, Hamilton, had a natural harbour most suitable for flying-boat operations.

This was not the case in New York, as there were no adequate bases suitable for flying-boat operations in the northeast coastal region of the United States. Pan American had to acquire its own base at Port Washington, Long Island, and in 1934 had negotiated with the city of Baltimore for the lease of a marine base there.

In May 1937, Captain Harold Gray made the first survey flight from Port Washington to Bermuda using an S-42B, while a reciprocal flight was made by Imperial Airways using a Short C-Class flying-boat. Apart from terminal facilities, Pan American constructed a fully equipped weather and radio station at Port Washington and in due course was to locate meteorologists at points in Newfoundland and Ireland.

Pan Am began regular scheduled passenger services on 18 June 1937 and Imperial Airways matched this with a reciprocal service. Then, in November, the S-42B *Bermuda Clipper* made its first flight from the new base at Baltimore. This service was to provide useful new experience for Pan Am and it gave an insight into foreign airline activities through its partnership with Imperial Airways; both airlines profited from the experience.

The C-Class flying-boat used by Imperial Airways was one of the latest types to be built by Short Brothers, then based at Rochester in England, and which would be used by the carrier on a number of Empire routes to Australia, South Africa and India. The British manufacturer Short Brothers had been making flying-boats since 1924 and the Short C-Class was its most modern type; the company shortly received an order from Imperial Airways for 28. Three of the type were to make experimental trans-Atlantic crossings in 1937 in conjunction with Pan American. One of them was lost in January 1939 due to icing.

REALISING A DREAM

For Trippe, who was overseeing all of these activities at the time, his long-held dream was becoming a reality. Pan American had flown the Pacific and it would now shortly fly the Atlantic. Harold Gray made the first survey flight to Bermuda and was followed by other pilots making survey flights across the Atlantic. Fitted with extra fuel tanks, an S-42B left the Port Washington harbour for Shediac, New Brunswick, on 25 June 1937. This 650-mile (1040-km) leg was the first on the proposed northern route, and the aircraft returned to New York the same day.

Two days later it left Port Washington for Botwood, Newfoundland, some 400 miles (640km) further northwest. The aircraft reached Botwood and flew back to New York two days later. On 3 July, the S-42B departed for Port Washington for Southampton, England, with stops at Shediac, Botwood and Foynes in southwest Ireland. This crossing covered a total distance of some 3500 miles (5600km) and took a flying time of 22 hours 39 minutes. It is on record as the first crossing of the North Atlantic by any commercial aeroplane. The flight followed the great circle route between New York and northwest

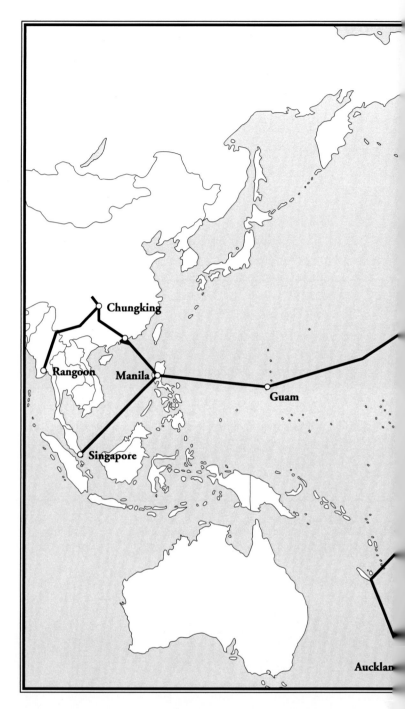

Europe and the trip was repeated a few days later, leaving New York on 28 July and arriving back on 7 August. Finally, on 16 August 1937, the S-42B left New York for Southampton by way of the southern route, calling at Bermuda, the Azores, Lisbon and Marseilles, returning to Port Washington on 3 September after its third trans-Atlantic round trip.

All the survey flights were incident-free, and Trippe was impatient for services to begin. A major problem was the suitability of the aeroplanes. The S-42Bs would be unsuitable for trans-Atlantic flights and the M-130s could also be ruled out as they were committed to the Pacific. Much depended upon the new Boeing flying-boats when they came into service.

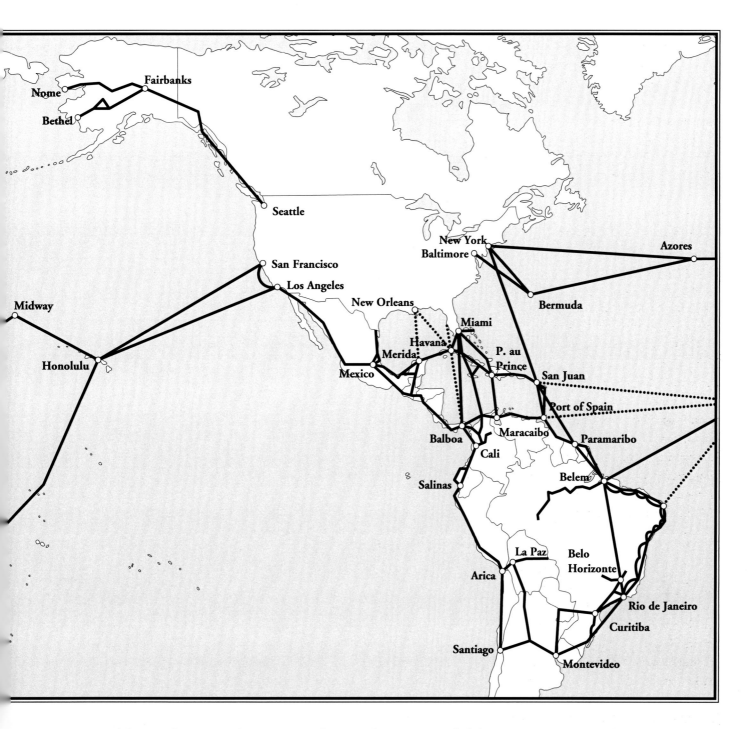

Meanwhile, consideration was being given to factors such as the weather conditions over the routes. Charles Lindbergh had concluded in his earlier surveys that the difficulties of the northern route had been exaggerated, although poor weather conditions which often prevailed had to be looked at closely. Fog and icing were matters that had never bothered Pan Am on its Central and South American services, and weather had given little cause for concern either on the trans-Pacific service. The North Atlantic could be another matter, and effective de-icing equipment was a necessary precaution. For the first time Pan Am fitted leading edge inflatable rubber de-icing boots to the wing and tail unit on the Sikorsky S-42Bs and propeller blade de-icers

were installed also. Pan Am's own meteorologists played a newly important role in providing weather maps for flight-planning on the routes. These depicted expected cloud conditions, temperature distribution and other information, enabling the aircraft to cross the ocean while avoiding icing as far as possible.

The newly established Atlantic Division now had a sizeable staff as it was gradually prepared for the new and exciting service. While Imperial Airways was also carrying out survey flights, gaining experience similar to Pan American, the airline was less ready than Pan Am and had a prime commitment to its Empire routes to Africa and Asia with the aircraft it had in hand. Trippe could not push things along any faster for Pan American.

The four Wright Double Cyclone engines of the B314 developed three times as much power as the S-38 and nearly twice that of the M-130.

CHAPTER NINE

Big Bold Boeing

As Trippe waited in 1937 for the first flight of the new Boeing flying-boat, traffic in mail and passengers was growing remarkably. That year mail and parcel loads leapt 25 per cent to a total of 2000 tonnes. The number of passengers carried totalled 214,000 and the route network now stretched to 50,695 miles (81,000km). The new Bermuda service contributed to this network expansion, and it seemed to Trippe that this was a natural outcome of the airline's growth: the more the airline did and the farther it stretched services the greater it grew. In the light of such results it was all too easy for Trippe to overreach himself.

The year 1938 dawned, and along with it came the start of many problems. Trippe was preoccupied with the Pacific routes and most importantly, development of his latest project the new flying-boat. Pan Am's engineers had prepared specifications for a follow-on aircraft to the Martin M-130 in 1935 and Trippe shortly invited various manufacturers to tender for the aircraft, which, it was made clear, should be a large, long-range aircraft suitable for over-ocean services. Glenn Martin was approached, but his design did not meet the specification. Douglas Aircraft expressed interest, but was already heavily committed to a landplane work programme. Boeing responded, and in the Spring of 1936 a Boeing design with the model number 314 was submitted to Trippe as a likely candidate. Boeing had been making flying-boats since 1920, but owed nothing to Pan American up to this point. Trippe liked the design of the 314 in every way, and a contract for six Boeing 314s was signed on 21 July 1936. On 7 June 1938, the first Boeing 314 was to make

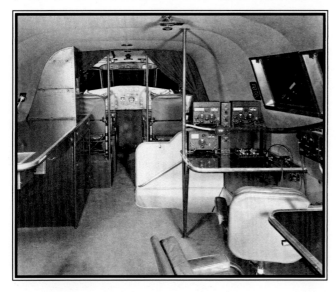

ABOVE *Re-fitted with triple fins and rudders, 18601 was christened* Honolulu Clipper *and was followed in this form by 11 more B314s.*

LEFT *Flight deck of the B314, showing the comfortable space for crew. The navigator's position is to the left, the radio operator's to the right. Note also the stairway down to the passenger deck.*

its maiden flight and Trippe was very anxious to see how the aircraft would perform.

THE ULTIMATE FLYING-BOAT

The Boeing 314 was the largest and most advanced airliner to be built in the United States to date, and it represented the ultimate in flying-boat design. The aircraft was a massive but also fine-looking machine, and before long it would make a major impact on the airline business. It had a wing span of 152ft (36m), a length of 106ft (32m) and a gross weight of 82,500lb (37,500kg). It had almost twice the power of the Martin M-130 and could carry 74 passengers and a crew of 10. The overall height was almost 28ft (8.5m) and the gross wing area was 2867ft² (266m²).

Because of its size, final assembly of the 314 was made outside the Boeing factory, and after launching into the adjacent Duwamish River the aircraft was towed down the river by barges to the Boeing test site, located among the shipyards in Elliot Bay, the seaport for Seattle.

When completed it would be the largest production aeroplane in airline service anywhere in the world. Like its recent flying-boat predecessors, the Boeing 314 had a boat-like hull fitted with the now familiar sponsons on either side of the lower fuselage, while the three-piece wing had its centre section built through the shoulder of the hull and its four powerful engines faired into the leading edge with long cowlings. In its initial form the 314 had a single fin and rudder surmounting the tailplane, but this was to change before long as it gave insufficient directional control and was replaced by a triple fin arrangement through the addition of two extra fins, one at either end of the tailplane. This arrangement gave greater side area and was to become the final design.

While the 314 had room for up to 74 passengers and a crew of ten, the arrangement varied in the usual way according to the nature of the flight. In the sleeper arrangement, forty passengers would be carried. The crew accommodation provided for a flight engineer station and crew sleeping quarters on a separate deck from the passengers, while the hull was of sufficient size to permit the passenger cabin to be divided into seven separate compartments, several having slightly different floor levels because of the slope of the bottom of the hull. Maximum range of the aircraft would be 3500 miles (5600km) and the cruising speed over this range would be 183mph (293kmh), the service ceiling of the aircraft would be 13,400ft (4060m) and the engines powering this heavy-weight new flying-boat would be Wright GR-2600 Double Cyclone 1200-hp engines, rated at 1500hp for take-off.

One of the novel features provided by the large, deep-chord wing was access to the four engines in flight and, by means of a companionway, the engineers could reach all fuel lines, control cables and the entire interior of the wing.

As Pan American was paying $550,700 each for the six Boeing 314s, Trippe made it clear to the company that he wanted unprecedented comfort and luxury for the passengers, and in this respect Boeing would not fail him. Boeing did not fall down on the other specifications either, for these included the efficient and safe operation of the aircraft in service, great ease of maintenance, ease of handling and minimum strain on the crew.

Due to its design, the 314 provided more volume for passengers and cargo than had previously been the case and this of course made the aircraft that much more comfortable for passengers and crew. Depending upon the nature of the service, the crew would be either nine or ten, with a standard crew of five flight-deck crew members and four pursers.

Each of the wing's sections held a fuel tank, while four other tanks were built into the sponsons. As with the Martin M-130s, the sponsons were used for lateral stability on the water, while they also served to carry fuel. They served also as short boarding ramps for passengers, as they could step directly from them through a door into the cabin. Made largely of metal throughout, the aircraft had fabric covered ailerons and flaps. Because of the long, non-stop distances on which the 314 would operate, provision was made for the carriage of two complete flight crews, but even this did not make the flight deck crowded as there was so much space. There was provision for two stewards on the flight deck, although these were usually busy on the passenger decks below.

The two pilots were positioned on the flight deck (in what had previously been the cockpit) and behind them sat the navigator on the port side, and opposite him sat the radio operator with his transmitters and receivers and direction-finding equipment. Between the co-pilot (or first officer) and the radio operator was a stairway leading down to the passenger deck. At the rear of the flight deck on the port side, was a further crew seat.

Behind the flight deck was a compartment for the crew which provided sleeping accommodation. Forward of the flight deck, and on the other side of the main bulkhead, was an equipment room for housing the mooring gear, additional bunks for crew sleeping and cargo and mail.

BELOW *Like a fish out of water, this Boeing 314 looks cumbersome and unhappy when removed from its natural environment – the sea.*

OCEAN LINER COMFORT

For the passengers, conditions were said to resemble more closely those of an ocean liner than for air travel, so luxurious and spacious were the arrangements devised by Boeing. The Pan Am order was a most important one for the company and Boeing, like Pan Am, wanted to be known for its superlative standards. With seven compartments to choose from, all with straight cabin walls and a flat ceiling, there was ample sitting and walking room for the passengers on long over-ocean flights. One of the compartments was set aside as a 14-seat dining room, and there was in addition a private suite in the extreme rear of the aircraft. Sleeping berth accommodation was provided for all passengers on trans-ocean flights.

The B314 introduced a number of firsts in passenger comfort, among them proper toilets for both men and women which could be discharged over the ocean. Passenger lounges were furnished with comfortable armchairs upholstered in wool tapestry and the materials covered 9000ft^2 (836m^2) of upholstery

ABOVE The NX registration on the wing signifies that the aircraft was still a prototype. A twin-finned version preceded the final three-fin arrangement.

and carpeting materials. Throughout the ship there were no less than 65 windows. The full service kitchen, or galley, produced the food which was served on real china. There was a bar where passengers could take drinks in flight.

For passenger safety, each aircraft carried eight ten-person life-rafts, enough life jackets for everyone on board, flare pistols, signal lights, emergency radios and buckets. Moreover, all the upholstery had been fireproofed, which was the first time a serious attempt had been made to incorporate fire-resistant cabin materials in an airliner.

One way and another, Boeing was breaking new ground with this remarkable aircraft and it was not surprising perhaps that when the B314 was in operational service the turn-around of an aircraft would involve 200 men making 1500 inspection

and servicing operations. Initially, six days would be needed for the entire operation, this being later reduced to four days and eventually 48 hours. Much was to come from such experience.

Delivery of the first aircraft had originally been scheduled for December 1937, but construction and development had taken much longer than expected and the test flying programme was to add more time to the introductory programme. The maiden flight of the first Boeing 314 was made on 7 June 1938 with Boeing's chief test pilot, Eddie Allen at the controls. The flight lasted 38 minutes. When the problem of lateral instability had been cured, by the addition of the triple-fin arrangement, the programme was continued until some 5000 miles (8000km) of in-flight trials were made. Flight tests showed that the Boeing flying-boat had a cruising speed of 150mph (240kmh) at 11,000ft (3330m) and would thereby meet the Pan American specification. Take-off speed was some 160 knots, or 180mph (288kmh). The approach to land was made at 103mph (165kmh).

All of this took months and the Civil Aeronautics Board did not grant an approved type certificate until 26 January 1939. Thus, Trippe was denied the pleasure of introducing the Boeing 314 into passenger service in 1938; but this would not have been possible anyway without receipt of the requisite landing permits from France and Portugal, which were still awaited.

By the end of 1938, Trippe had much more to worry about as he fought to stay at the helm of the airline he had built.

BELOW *NC 18605 became* Dixie Clipper. *It inaugurated the first trans-Atlantic passenger service from New York to Marseilles on 28 June 1939.*

Final assembly of the Boeing 314 had to be done outside the factory, as with the M-130,
and the aircraft was then floated on the river.

CHAPTER TEN

The Magnificent Long Jump

Smarting at his new, lowly position, Trippe took some comfort in the first months of 1939 from the fact that Boeing's new flying-boat would soon be carrying the Pan Am title to more distant parts of the world. Following the grant of its type certificate on 26 January, the first Boeing 314 was delivered to Pan American Airways on 27 January 1939, and for good measure Boeing delivered the second aircraft on the same day. These bore the construction numbers NC 18601 and NC 18602. While the Atlantic beckoned, the Pacific was by now badly in need of additional trans-ocean aircraft and both of these aircraft were placed in service in the Pacific. The remaining four were delivered in February, March and June of 1939. By June of that year the momentous achievement of the first scheduled passenger services across the North Atlantic would be reached.

In January 1939, authority was finally granted by the French government for operating rights, and this was followed by the Portuguese government confirming permission for Pan American to operate to the Azores and Lisbon. The way was now clear for some positive action. On 4 February, the Atlantic Division received its first Boeing 314 (NC 18603) and a week later, on 3 March, it was named *Yankee Clipper* by Mrs Eleanor Roosevelt, wife of the president, at an impressive ceremony at the Anacostia Naval Air Station in Washington DC. After some preparation, the *Yankee Clipper* was flown on 26 March 1939

ABOVE *The second B314 flying-boat delivered, the* California Clipper *was used in the Pacific. Many people in this crowd were Pan Am's own support workers watching proceedings.*

by Captain Harold Gray, now head of the Atlantic Division, on a survey flight to Europe by way of the southern route, that is, Baltimore–Azores–Lisbon–Marseilles. On this flight there were 21 people on board including the crew and observers from the US Government and Pan American's operations department.

By now Pan Am had moved its Atlantic Division headquarters from Port Washington to Baltimore, just north of Washington DC. On the outward trip on 26 March, *Yankee Clipper* was flown non-stop from Baltimore to the Azores, a distance of some 2500 miles (4000km). The aircraft was back at its base on 19 April after an incident-free double Atlantic crossing.

This survey flight was so satisfactory that preparations were made for the commencement of scheduled services. These would begin with a mail-carrying flight, and, on 20 May 1939, 1800lb (820kg) of mail was loaded on to the *Yankee Clipper,* and under the command of Captain Arthur LaPorte the world's first trans-Atlantic scheduled air-mail service was begun, on the southern route to Lisbon and Marseille, in the scheduled time of 29 hours. On 24 June the same aircraft, commanded by Captain Gray, opened the northern mail route to Southampton, England, by way of Shediac, Botwood, and Foynes, Ireland. The fourth Boeing 314, named *Atlantic*

Clipper, had been delivered on 20 March 1939 and on 17 June, piloted by Captain Wallace Culbertson, this aircraft made a route-proving flight carrying 16 members of the press.

By now Europe-bound passengers, who had been waiting for long months, had been alerted by Pan American that their long-held reservations would shortly be effected and they were excitedly standing by. On 28 June 1939, the dream was realised for all concerned when *Dixie Clipper,* commanded by Captain Rod Sullivan, opened the first trans-Atlantic passenger service, carrying 22 passengers. The aircraft flew from New York down to Marseilles, and with this flight and the previous mail-carrying flights Pan American went down in air transport history as the first to make scheduled commercial services across the Atlantic. Trippe was said not to be on the *Dixie Clipper* for this first flight.

The *Yankee Clipper* opened the northern service on 8 July, carrying 17 passengers. The sixth B314 of this initial fleet was delivered in June and Pan American was now strongly

ABOVE *Radio operator and flight engineers' stations on a B314.*

LEFT *Pan Am was a driving force behind developments in navigation using such techniques as radio direction finding, as can be seen on this B314.*

placed to carry passengers and mail routinely on this luxury flying-boat service. Apart from that fact, Pan Am had beaten Imperial Airways in the achievement of a trans-Atlantic service. Thereafter, services were maintained at a weekly frequency on both the northern and southern routes, the former terminating at Southampton and the latter at Marseilles. Both Imperial Airways and Air France began trans-Atlantic operations a little after Pan American, but Pan Am was the only carrier to carry passengers on trans-Atlantic services until World War II began in Europe, on 3 September 1939.

A SHORT-LIVED LEAD

Passengers flocked to the new Boeing service and Pan Am was the toast of the airline industry. This was a valuable service and a remarkable one, and while the fares were expensive there was no shortage of customers. From New York across the Atlantic the standard one-way fare was $375 and $675 return.

For this, passengers experienced the most comfortable flight in luxurious surroundings, lasting not much more than a day and a night, and where watchful pursers were always on hand to tend to their every need.

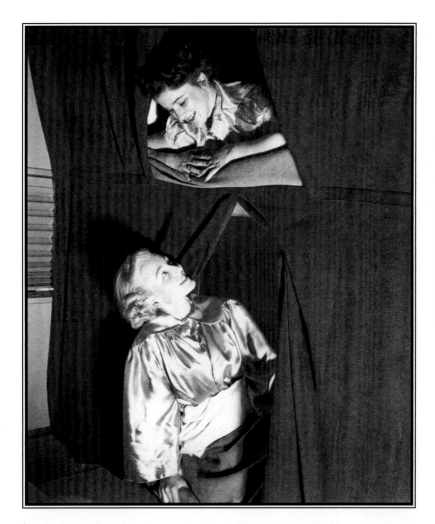

ABOVE *The B314 engines could be reached for servicing from both outside the engines and internally through the massive deep-chord wing.*

LEFT *Sweet dreams. In the sleeper configuration, the B314 could accommodate up to 40 passengers. There was also a honeymoon suite.*

The 12½-ft (3.8-m) wide cabin provided more passenger space than any commercial aeroplane in service and the B314 could rightly be described as the world's first 'wide-body'. Boeing was to maintain then – as it would thirty years later with the Boeing 747 (cabin width of 20ft [6m]) – that the key to such comfort was space. This was partly provided by the twin decks, one for the passengers and the other for crew (the B747 was to repeat the formula). Innovative use of space provided room for everyone to move and at the same time enjoy this wonderful experience. In short, the Boeing 314s were high-flying hotels and the standards unexcelled.

Each passenger was given a complete formal table setting for meals, which were prepared on board in the large forward galley. A typical dinner would comprise shrimp cocktail, turtle soup, steak, mashed potatoes, asparagus, salad, peach melba and petits fours, accompanied by French wines, champagne and a wide choice of other drinks. Breakfast more often than not included fresh strawberries and cream. The stewards would prepare all food for consumption on board.

After flying through the night in a comfortable, if size-limited, sleeping bunk, passengers would find their shoes cleaned and polished when they awoke.

John Salmini and Bruce Candotti had been trained as chefs by New York's Waldorf Hotel, but were two among many to be recruited by Pan Am as pursers. They were hired expressly to plan, prepare and serve meals which would satisfy the tastes of passengers, many of whom would be connoisseurs of good food.

It would have been surprising if the B314s had been totally trouble-free and there were of course minor problems, mainly regarding the engines and systems. The propellers gave problems initially, proving very noisy, but this was solved by the makers cutting 4½in (11.4cm) off each blade tip.

When Trippe had placed his order for a first six back in July 1936, he had placed an option on a further six and this was converted into a firm order in the summer of 1939. At that point the opportunity was taken to specify a number of improvements to the aircraft, which would increase the gross take-off weight by 1500lb (680kg) to 84,000lb (37,800kg) or 42 tonnes. The fuel tankage was also increased from 4200 to 5448 US gallons (15,920 to 20,650 litres). Additionally, more powerful Wright Double Cyclone R-2600A engines gave 1600hp compared with the previous 1500hp. Also, the interior arrangements were revised somewhat. These later models were to be known as B314A, and in this version, the large flying-boat could carry 35 to 40 passengers over 1500-mile (2415-km) stages on trans-Atlantic operations. Cruising speed, however, was still fairly modest at 150mph (240kmh).

This happy state of affairs continued for just three months more until war in Europe began in September 1939. Pan Am maintained its schedules until 1 September, but the effect on trans-Atlantic services was immediate. On 3 October, Pan Am formally suspended its passenger services to Marseilles and Southampton, but service was maintained into Europe by way of the southern route, terminating at Lisbon, on a twice-weekly schedule. This was possible because Portugal remained neutral; the service was maintained until 1942.

MEETING DEMAND

When it was known that the flying-boat service was to be carried on, demand for seats on the Atlantic services immediately soared, especially from Europe to America. In the absence of an official priority system Pan American had to devise one of its own. On these flights, loads sometimes reached a maximum of 13,620lb (6200kg). In the first winter of trans-Atlantic operations weather conditions proved exceptionally harsh, and with severe icing being encountered along the northeast US coast the terminating points were moved from Port Washington and Baltimore down to Miami. Weather conditions of such a severe kind had not been expected, and ice at the northerly points became so much of a problem that flights sometimes had to be cancelled. Heavy seas in the Azores were also a problem and in November 1939 five of the eleven trips operated were delayed for two or more days because of bad weather. During the period December 1939 to April 1940 only 60 per cent of the 87 trans-Atlantic trips scheduled were completed, and of these many were delayed for periods ranging from a day to up to two weeks.

On 31 March 1940, Atlantic operations were transferred to a new terminal at La Guardia, New York, and a month later the

BELOW *In its developed version, the B314 weighed almost 42 tonnes. Demand for seats on the truncated service was massive right from the outset.*

services were increased to three round trips a week, although this was still only meeting a fraction of the demand. In 1940, Pan American carried some 30 per cent of all trans-Atlantic mail.

The basic services to Lisbon were not enough to do Pan American very much good, for they were a shadow of what had been originally planned and while Pan American was still showing its colours on both sides of the Atlantic, the service was generating little revenue for the airline. The intention had been to increase frequencies and in due course add services to other destinations in Europe, but this was not possible with a limited fleet operating on one route only.

The curtailment of the Atlantic services by the war was perhaps the deepest cut of all, and it seemed as though it was yet another of the blows Pan American had suffered over the previous two years. While Pan American was on the lips of everyone in aviation, people were generally unaware that the airline was beset by such problems. A good income would be needed before long to not only write-off the capital costs of the Boeing 314s but to invest for the post-war period and future aircraft.

NO WAR FOR THE US

To finance the purchase of the Boeing 314s, Pan American had issued Trust Notes at an interest rate of four per cent per annum, and to gain needed capital in 1940 Pan American issued stock to the amount of $6.3 million. This was substantial

Boeing B-314 Clipper

1 1600-hp Wright Double Cyclone engines
2 Cockpit
3 Radio Officer's station
4 Baggage compartment, crew quarters (to rear)
5 Lounge
6 Deluxe Suite
7 Women's dressing room
8 Cabins converted for sleeping
9 Dining room/lounge
10 Stabiliser/fuel reservoir
11 Lounge
12 Dressing room
13 Staircase to flight deck, bar & galley (behind)
14 Passenger lounge
15 Crew's day cabin

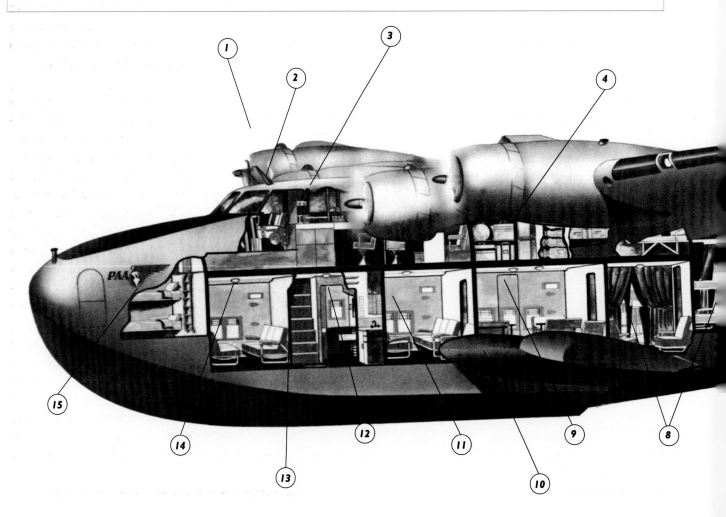

but it would be insignificant in comparison to the sums needed for aircraft after the war.

At that point, however, the United States was not involved in the European war and there were many strong voices in the country arguing for staying out of it. Among them was Charles Lindbergh, who advocated isolationism and who would shortly be a leading figure in the America First organisation. President Roosevelt, however, was increasingly alarmed by Germany's imperialistic ambitions and noted with dismay developments in Europe that had caused Pan American to abandon its only recently begun trans-Atlantic air services.

In spite of the on-going struggle, the year 1939 was a successful year for Pan American financially, and with the Central and Latin American services, coupled with the Pacific services, revenue had been steadily coming in. After the bad year of 1938, 1939 produced a profit of $1,984,438 after taxes, on an operating revenue of $20,610,930. The airline was still heavily reliant on mail revenue, however, and the contribution that year exceeded $11 million. A turn-around in the Pacific services had come about as a result of the increase in the mail rates per aircraft mile.

In 1940 the sun shone again for Juan Trippe, as the board reinstated him to his previous executive position. It had become well aware that Pan American was much the poorer without his business acumen and technical understanding. Sonny §Whitney may well have had banking skills, but he was no airline entrepreneur.

The question now was where did Pan Am go next?

ABOVE *This cutaway diagram shows the internal layout of the Boeing B314 Clipper, used by Pan American throughout the 1930s and 1940s.*

The Boeing 314 would establish many records, among them the first trans-Atlantic air-mail service and the first trans-Atlantic passenger service.

War All Over

In 1940, Franklin Roosevelt was re-elected as President of the United States for yet a third term and within a few months he had introduced into law a Lend-Lease Act which would mean that military materials and aid could be supplied to the United Kingdom. While Roosevelt had maintained in his campaign that he would keep the United States out of war, he had seen in the summer of 1940 the collapse of France, Belgium, Holland and other European countries to Hitler's forces, and he understood that if Britain went the same way there would be virtual domination of Europe by Hitler's Reich.

The US government's sympathetic attitude towards Britain was manifest in some early contracts. These had nothing to do with Pan American's aircraft at this stage, but rather the construction of air bases, at which Pan American had already gained much expertise. In November 1940, a subsidiary of Pan American Airways, the Pan American Airport Construction Corporation, signed a contract with the British government for the construction of a number of airfields in the Caribbean area. A number of bases in British territory were turned over to the US government in exchange for fifty destroyers, which could be used to augment the hard-pressed Royal Navy Fleet.

Then, on 11 November 1940, the first Atlantic ferry operation was undertaken by the Canadian Pacific Railway Air Service, which saw the first flights of aeroplanes for Britain and which were made in US factories. In June 1941, ferrying operations were made directly from the United States by Atlantic Airways, a company jointly owned by Pan American and British Overseas Airways Corporation (BOAC). This

ABOVE *Passengers embarking for the first trans-Atlantic passenger service, from New York to Marseilles, on 28 June 1939. The aircraft is the* Dixie Clipper.

operation involved the flying of aircraft to Africa by the southern route, across the South Atlantic.

In mid-1940, the Director General of BOAC (which had succeeded Imperial Airways on 1 April 1940 as the reconstituted state airline) was anxious about the airline's fleet, which was already being turned over to war-time needs. He pressed the Air Ministry for additional aircraft with long ranges and requested the use of five flying-boats and some nine landplanes, making the point that US civil aircraft appeared to be the only types adequate for BOAC's needs. The upshot of this was that three Boeing 314A flying-boats were purchased from Pan American with the US government's backing. The first of these, NC 18607, was delivered to BOAC in May 1941. The two others, NC 18608 and NC18610, followed in May and June of that year respectively.

Poor Pan American! Not only was the airline losing grasp of the blue riband it had so successfully won for the trans-Atlantic services, but now the airline was giving up three of its fleet to its great rival, Britain's state airline. Everyone understood, however, that Britain's need at that point was far greater than that of Pan American's, and it would not be too long anyway before the whole of the remaining 314 clipper fleet would be turned over to the US government.

Meanwhile, BOAC repainted the aircraft in full British camouflage and re-christened them respectively *Bristol*, *Berwick* and *Bangor* for initial service on the trans-Atlantic route, which the airline carried on from Southampton and Poole to the United States by way of Foynes in neutral Ireland.

THE VIEWS OF THE CHIEF

The thoughts in the mind of Pan American's chief architect at that uncertain time will never be known, but the high regard in which Trippe was held was reflected in an invitation he received in mid-1941 from the Royal Aeronautical Society of Britain, the oldest aeronautical society in the world. Trippe was asked to give the 29th Wilbur Wright Memorial Lecture, with his subject as 'Ocean Air Transport', and on 17 June 1941 he found himself in war-shattered Britain describing what had been achieved.

Speaking as he said he did for the 7000 men and women who constituted the Pan American Airways System, Trippe reminded his audience that it was only in October 1927 that the first Pan American scheduled air service was inaugurated, over the 100-mile (160-km) stretch between Key West, Florida and Havana, Cuba. From the first he had seen that the pleasures and values of such operations quickly broke down prevailing public resistance to over-water flying, and Pan American had gone on to conquer the Pacific and now the Atlantic. The pioneering efforts had been long and hard but were worth it in every respect.

Pointing out that in its brief history air transportation had been confronted not only with great technical problems, but also complicated political problems, Trippe noted that there was no real 'freedom of the air', for every country now claimed full sovereignty over its air space. Before air transport operations could be enacted between the United States and Europe, many of these political questions had to be settled, and it was not until 1937 that sufficient progress in the solution of the problems had been achieved to permit the start of flights.

From an operating point of view, the Atlantic had lived up to its advance reputation and it was fair to say that the difficulties encountered were sufficient to confirm the North Atlantic as being technically the most difficult of any major aerial trade route. Flight logs had shown how difficult the operations were through the winter of 1939–40. Many flights were delayed due to harbour conditions at the base at Horta, in the Azores. Others were cancelled due to extremely strong westerly winds, and unflyable mid-ocean storms covered areas too wide to detour. Still others flown were able to carry only very limited westbound payloads. In the winter of 1940–41

ABOVE *First-class service and facilities added to the glamour and excitement of Clipper Ship travel.*

LEFT *A radio officer, responsible for operation of the plane's complete radio equipment, at work on the Boeing 314.*

RIGHT *Venetian blinds, reading lights and well-upholstered seats were all part of the comfort enjoyed by passengers on the B314.*

another route had been surveyed as a consequence which swung far south from the usual route. Heading south from Lisbon, the Clippers landed at Bolama in Portuguese Guinea, then turned westward to Belem in Brazil and thence northward to New York by way of Trinidad and either Puerto Rico or Bermuda. Such a route was 4085 miles (6535km) longer than the Lisbon–Azores–Bermuda–New York route and correspondingly more expensive to operate. Nevertheless, said Trippe, it increased the number of passengers and mails moved from Europe to the United States. By overflying Horta on eastbound trips, Clippers were able to complete 50 per cent more crossings than during the previous winter. From a total of 25 trips scheduled in the three winter months of 1940, only 14 had been completed. In 1941, 21 of these flights were completed by way of the southern route – an 84 per cent performance record against 56 per cent for the previous year. Where traffic was concerned, the route was equally satisfactory, for in the winter of 1940 only 286

people were carried from Lisbon to New York. In the winter of 1941 this total reached 471 for the same period, and this in spite of an increase in mail loads.

VISION AND INNOVATION

Trippe continued with his account, relating that many innovations had first been introduced by Pan American, and among others was the development of the Multiple Flight Crew. This specialised arrangement, and the training that went with it, meant that it had been possible to conduct flights as long as 24 hours in duration. The Multiple Flight Crew had been adopted as standard with the inception of four-engined operations, as these had shown that there was a need for larger crews, individually trained for specialised duties.

The Multiple Flight Crew comprised a captain and specialist officers directly responsible to him for piloting, navigation, engineering, communications and passenger service. Each of

ABOVE *Pan Am publicised that it happily served passengers of all ages.*

LEFT *The arrival of* Dixie Clipper *at Marseilles, June 1939.*

these had a qualified assistant capable of relieving him for rest periods. A Clipper captain was the chief administrative officer, who was invariably a veteran of many years of experience on Pan American's overseas flights. In addition, he had qualified through research and study, to attain the rank of Master of Ocean Flying-Boats. This meant that he was qualified in aeronautical engineering, engine and aeroplane mechanics, in meteorology and radio operation, while he also held the equivalent of a Master Mariners ticket. It also meant that he was qualified in the subject of international law, marine law and business administration. The flight engineer was responsible for the mechanical operation of the aircraft and the power plants. The flight radio officer was responsible for the operation of the plane's complete radio equipment and for maintenance of constant communications with the radio control stations ashore. The third officer, who was a junior pilot-in-training, served primarily as relief for the second officer during the flight,

while the fourth officer, also a junior pilot, assisted pilot officers in both flight and ground duties. There was an assistant flight engineer, an assistant flight radio officer and the flight steward, whose duties included responsibility for all details related to the comfort of passengers; he had an assistant flight steward.

For trans-Atlantic flights it had been necessary to devise an easily usable yardstick of performance, and for this Pan American had developed what it called the 'Howgozit Curve'. The Howgozit Curve was developed by the ocean captains under the leadership of Captain Harold Gray, and its purpose was to present to the crew and the flight watch ashore a continuous flow of information as to the fuel reserve remaining on board the aircraft and the fuel required for completion of the flight to destination, or back to the point of departure.

It actually consisted of five curves which were required to clearly present this picture. The curve of miles versus gallons was plotted showing normal four-engine fuel consumption for the flight in progress. The second curve showed gallons versus hours of flying. The third curve was of hours versus miles. The fourth and fifth curves showed miles versus gallons, which were also plotted for three-engine conditions in the event that that might be necessary. Trippe was not to know that the Howgozit Chart would come to be a standard aid in airline operations in the years ahead.

Trippe noted the requirement for continued research into aircraft and other technical concerns. The aeroplanes of the time, he averred, were far from what he would call the 'ideal trans-Atlantic aircraft' and he thought it would be many years before depreciation and not obsolescence would be Pan American's concern. He thought substantial advancement of ocean air transport should by no means be dependent upon further revolutionary developments, but rather refinement of details to produce far-reaching results.

The need for efficiency distinguished the long-range ocean transport from other civil aircraft. For example, the latest type of short-range landplane could make a flight of 750 miles (1200km), with 45 minutes' fuel reserve, carrying a full load of 21 passengers. If some means could be found to increase the efficiency of this aircraft by one per cent this would increase its payload by only 27lb (12kg). If a corresponding increase of one per cent could be made to the efficiency of the Boeing 314, there would be a gain of no less than 240lb (109kg), or slightly more than the allowance for one passenger. Effort and expense, concluded Trippe, were justified for continuing research whereby such efficiency improvements could be achieved.

Perhaps with an eye on the remarkable distance his airline had come in just 14 years, Trippe offered a final comment before his large and distinguished audience: 'With future advances in the offing who would be bold enough to predict the distant future?'

Unfortunately for Trippe and Pan American, it would be some years before the airline could regain its stride in civil operations, for in less than six months the world would have another war on its hands as Japan attacked the United States at Pearl Harbor.

PAN AM GOES TO WAR

On 7 December 1941, the day of the attack, Pan American entered the war proper, in common with all US airlines. The remaining nine Boeing 314s were immediately drafted into the US Army and Navy; four of these were shortly to be returned to Pan American but remained under US Navy control. On 7 December the *Anzac Clipper* (NC 18611 delivered in June 1941) was one hour out of Pearl Harbor on an otherwise routine flight from San Francisco to Hawaii. The radio suddenly came to life with the agitated voice of the Hawaiian air controller. 'We are under attack,' he said, 'this is not a drill, Pan Am. I repeat we are under attack'. The aircraft was put into a sharp bank and diverted to the larger island of Hilo 200 miles (320km) away where it immediately elected to return to San Francisco. Another of Pan Am's flying-boats, the Martin M-130 named *Philippine Clipper* had just left Wake Island. It returned to pick up all the American staff and, although shot at by the Japanese, carried them safely back to Honolulu. The Sikorsky S-42 *Hong Kong Clipper* was not so lucky and was destroyed at its base in Hong Kong the following day when the Japanese attacked the British Colony.

The same morning another Boeing 314, the *Pacific Clipper* (NC 18609), was approaching Auckland, New Zealand, when a coded bulletin was received which said that war had broken out, and the aircraft should proceed to Auckland and await further instructions. Several days later the commander, Captain Robert Ford, was ordered with his 11-man crew to proceed to New York on a westbound course. This meant he had to fly from Auckland to Sydney, on to Surabaya, Trincomalee, Karachi,

Bahrain, Khartoum, Leopoldville, Natal and Port of Spain, maintaining strict radio silence throughout. Robert Ford and his crew made history with the flight for it covered 31,500 miles (50,710km) and was the first to be made completely around the world by a commercial aircraft.

On 12 December 1941, the US Assistant Secretary for War called on the airlines for the transport of vital men and materials, and the first agreement was made with Pan Am to extend its services through Africa to Teheran, Iran. As with the Boeing 314s, the remaining two Martin M-130s were to be turned over to the government but could be operated on its behalf by Pan Am.

Pan American continued its war service diligently and energetically, with the flying-boat fleet of S-42s, M-130s and

ABOVE *The B314 flying-boats served the Pan American Pacific routes well, until the Japanese declared war on the United States in 1941.*

B314s taking on a heavy share of the workload. The flying-boats carried government personnel, mail, medicines and essential military passengers, not to mention plasma, crude rubber, mica, beryllium and secret items of equipment. They were to maintain essential communication links to allied nations all over the world. It was said that Pan American's contribution to the United States war effort was unmatched.

All the harder for Pan American then was the acceptance of another airline authorised to operate trans-Atlantic services in 1942. American Export Lines, a shipping company, had formed an airline, American Export Airlines (AEA), in 1937 and had applied to the US government for permission to operate a trans-Atlantic route to England and France. Pan American had long argued against these permits, in particular the granting of mail contracts, and for a variety of reasons the arguments dragged on for some five years until in February 1942 American Export Airlines was given a temporary certificate to fly from New York to Foynes, Ireland.

AEA ordered three new flying-boats from Sikorsky, the VS-44, and services were inaugurated with these aircraft on 20 June 1942. AEA signed a contract with the US Naval Air Transport service and this service was carried on for the navy until 31 December 1944.

After the war AEA merged with American Airlines, when its name was changed to American Overseas Airlines Inc. By 1948, however, a very strong Pan American was in an aggressive

LEFT *The wing design for the B314 was in fact derived from that of a predecessor, the Boeing B-15 bomber, which was later developed into the B17.*

mood again under the authority of Trippe, and a merger was proposed. Pan American finally took over American Overseas Airlines on 25 September 1950.

A SEAL OF APPROVAL

On the day following the attack on Pearl Harbor, Britain's Prime Minister, Winston Churchill, decided to go to Washington following a telephone conversation with President Roosevelt. The sea voyage took eight days in weather conditions which were so bad that at one stage one of the party, Lord Beaverbrook, the Minister of Aircraft Production, complained that he might as well have gone by submarine. Following his meetings with Roosevelt and others, Churchill travelled by train to Ottawa to address the Canadian Parliament, thereafter returning to Washington for the journey home.

The British battleship *Duke of York* awaited Churchill's party in Bermuda harbour, along with an accompanying flotilla of escorting destroyers. For the journey to Bermuda one of Pan Am's Boeing 314s had been placed at his disposal. Churchill greatly enjoyed the flight, and was so impressed with the flying-boat that he asked the BOAC pilot, Captain Kelly Rogers,

BELOW *The California Clipper was the second Boeing 314 delivered to Pan American, in January 1939, and was later renamed* Pacific Clipper.

whether the aircraft could fly from Bermuda to England, the answer being an excited 'Yes!' With the prospect of a 40-mph (64-kmh) tail wind the flight could be made in 20 hours.

So much was going on in the world that Churchill thought the time-saving would be well worth it. After discussions with his companions, Churchill elected to make the flight. 'There is no doubt about the comfort of these great flying-boats', he is on record as saying. The flight was smooth, the high-priority passengers passed an agreeable afternoon and had 'a merry dinner'.

In not much more than a tenth of the time it would have taken for the sea journey, Churchill and his party were transported home to Plymouth harbour in fresh condition. In June 1942, he travelled to Washington again and this time there was no question in Churchill's mind as to the mode of travel he would take. Because of the urgency of war affairs he chose to fly, which meant that he would be cut off from information channels for no more than 24 hours, and again, Captain Kelly Rogers carried the party in a Boeing 314.

In January 1943, it was the turn of President Roosevelt to sample the Boeing 314, when the *Dixie Clipper* flew him to North Africa for the historic Casablanca Summit meeting with Churchill and Russia's Joseph Stalin. While the flying-boat was working for the US government it was crewed throughout by Pan American personnel and carried the airline's original civil registration number instead of military markings. In more ways

ABOVE *On his 61st birthday, President Franklin D. Roosevelt was presented with a cake on his flight to North Africa for the Casablanca Summit.*

than one, this flight was historic because it was the first flight outside the United States by an American president.

Many other VIPs and high-profile passengers were transported in this war-time period on what were essentially Pan American services, among them Queen Wilhelmina of the Netherlands, who left her beleaguered country for Canada, flying by way of Ireland to New Brunswick; Britain's Ambassador to Washington, Lord Halifax; Lord and Lady Mountbatten and numerous others, including General George C. Marshall who, in 1942, on a priority mission, was flown from Baltimore to Scotland on the first non-stop trans-oceanic passenger flight.

A HEAVY PRICE

War was now going on all over the world and it took its toll on Pan American's fleet. The S-42B *Hong Kong Clipper* had been destroyed at its moorings in Hong Kong at the start of the Japanese war. Another S-42B was lost in Brazil in 1943, as was an S-42 in Cuba in August 1944, while the three original S-40s were scrapped as by now having served their purpose.

One of the two remaining Martin M-130s crashed into a mountain north of San Francisco in January 1943 in bad weather, killing all of its crew of nine and ten passengers. This left the remaining M-130, the *China Clipper*, which continued in US Navy service until October 1943, whereafter it flew in Pan American service again until January 1945, when it was lost at Port of Spain, Trinidad.

On 22 February 1943 the Boeing 314 *Yankee Clipper* crashed on landing in the River Tagus, Lisbon, on a scheduled

ABOVE *On his 61st birthday, President Franklin D. Roosevelt was presented with a cake on his flight to North Africa for the Casablanca Summit.*

flight from La Guardia Marine Terminal, killing 24 of the 39 people on board. The fact that this was adjudged due to pilot error in the accident investigation simply piled on the agony for Pan American. Captain Sullivan in command had banked too sharply to port on his landing approach and hit the water with the wing tip, which broke up the wing and wrecked the aircraft.

The war-time flights continued, with good work being done by a reduced flying-boat fleet. This work took many forms, for example, in August 1942 the B314 *Anzac Clipper* was flying off of the African coast when it spotted a lifeboat carrying survivors from a sunken ship. It circled the lifeboat, noted and reported its position to the authorities and dropped food and water for the survivors on the return flight. In October 1943, one of the Clippers was sent to England on a special mission flight carrying four tonnes of maps and charts for the start of a new bombing programme in Europe.

President Roosevelt died suddenly in April 1945 and was succeeded by his vice-president, Harry Truman. Before long Truman would recognise the remarkable work that Pan American had performed during the war, and in 1946 he presented the Harmon Aviation Trophy to Juan Trippe, in recognition of the airline's contribution to the military success of the allied powers.

The Atlantic Clipper *was among those B314s taken over by the US government for war needs.*
Note the US flag – America had just 48 states at that time.

CHAPTER TWELVE

Days of Reflection

The war in Europe ended on 8 May 1945 and the war in the Far East finished on 2 September with the formal surrender of Japan. Some of Pan American's Clippers were already flying again with the airline and the *Atlantic, Dixie, American* and *Cape Town Clippers* were shortly de-commissioned by the US Navy. They had logged an impressive record during the war-time period. Overall they made 3000 crossings of the Atlantic, carried 80,000 passengers and flew approximately 11 million miles (almost 18 million km), a distance equivalent to 440 times around the world. It was a changing world, however, and while the flying-boats had been the medium by which Pan American had spread its global wings and made the airline the master of the skies, the beautiful ships were outmoded and needed to give way to new technology, which meant landplanes.

THE RISE OF THE LANDPLANE

The landplane had begun its rise to eminence in pre-war America and military needs had spurred this development. Transport aircraft, such as the Lockheed Constellation and Douglas DC-4, were already flying and now had a wealth of land airports and aerodromes available to them in different countries all over the world. The war had seen a vast airport building programme in which Pan Am itself played a strong part (constructing no less than fifty in different regions), and now capital cities could be reached by US and European airlines with little difficulty.

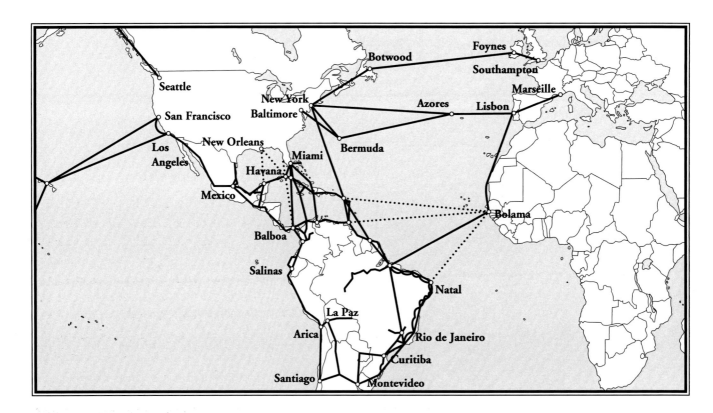

ABOVE *Map showing the proliferation of Pan American airline routes. Dotted lines indicate projected routes.*

LEFT *Three B314s were bought from Pan Am by Britain's BOAC.*

BELOW *The war over, the B314 was to fly in Pan Am colours for only a further year.*

Other factors had made their impression. The landplane was faster than the flying-boat by virtue of its fuselage design, could carry comparable fuel and better payloads and, while bad weather conditions such as fog would give problems for many years to come, the landplane had no difficulties with iced-up harbours or difficult sea conditions of the kind Trippe had described four years earlier. Probably nothing could better illustrate the problems of water operations than the sad end of the Boeing 314 *Honolulu Clipper*. The first B314 constructed and delivered to Pan Am, the *Honolulu Clipper* was on a scheduled flight from Honolulu to San Francisco in November 1945 when it suffered the loss of two engines, necessitating it to land on the sea. All passengers and crew were taken off safely, but it was not possible to repair the aircraft at sea because of the technical problems and a US Navy ship undertook to tow the flying-boat back to Honolulu. The sea became so rough, however, that the aircraft became damaged in collision with the tow ship and had to be

sunk by gunfire because of its unseaworthy state and danger to shipping. Nothing like this had happened before to any flying-boat, but the incident only served to emphasise the declining prospects for the flying-boat as a type.

American Overseas Airlines was the first to operate a scheduled landplane commercial flight across the Atlantic on

23 October 1945, when a DC-4 flew from New York to Hurn Airport, Bournemouth, England, by way of Gander and Shannon in Ireland. Pan American quickly followed on 27 October with its own DC-4 flight carrying 44 passengers. The aircraft cruised at 234 mph (374kmh), flew at 10,000ft (3000m) and had a 2250-mile (3600-km) range.

Pan Am ordered an initial fleet of 45 DC-4s and would subsequently increase this to some eighty aircraft. Pan Am was already operating landplanes and had been on some internal routes since the commencement of its services, and the airline was not to be left behind now. On 28 November 1945, Pan American ordered 20 Stratocruisers, a new commercial aircraft from Boeing, which had evolved from the wartime B29 bomber and thence to the C97 military transport. In due course, Pan Am would become the largest user of Stratocruisers, operating 29 in total.

On 14 January 1946, the Lockheed Constellation made its début on Pan Am's trans-Atlantic routes, and this was the largest and fastest commercial aircraft in service at the time. The Constellation had a pressurised cabin, enabling it to fly at 20,000ft (6060m) without causing passenger discomfort and a cruising speed of 300mph (480kmh). It would not be long before a later model, the Super Constellation with even longer range and more powerful engines would join Pan Am's fleet. On 17 June 1947, this occurred when the airline inaugurated a round-the-world service. On 29 August 1947, Pan Am commenced a scheduled, non-stop service between New York and London with this type.

The flying-boat was fading from the scene, although Pan American was to retain the name of Clipper for its future airliners. There was a brief burst of activity when the British company, Saunders-Roe, produced the Princess, a massive and beautiful flying-boat to specifications drawn by the war-time Brabazon Committee, but this ended in failure.

Powered by eight engines and capable of carrying two hundred passengers, three Princesses were built for BOAC's post-war needs. Unfortunately, the engines were a long-running problem and by the late 1950s the scene had totally changed and the landplane was the natural choice for BOAC, Pan American and all airlines. A number of offers were made for the Princess fleet, however the three completed aircraft were scrapped in 1967.

In the United States, the $40-million Hercules, created by the millionaire aviator and film magnate Howard Hughes and shipping tycoon Henry Kayser, was flown once (by Hughes) and thereafter put into permanent storage until it, too, was broken up. Capable of carrying 700 troops, the Hercules was a war-time project and could never have served Pan American in the post-war world. The flying-boat was a product of a past era and had been left behind by circumstances and technical developments. Pan Am recognised this even as the war was ending.

THE END OF AN ERA

On 6 January 1946, Pan Am operated the Boeing 314s for the final time on the Atlantic routes and, on 8 April 1946, the airline made its last B314 flight, on the Hawaii service. In January 1946, the Dinner Key flying-boat base at Miami was closed, but it was decided to retain the main aircraft and engine overhaul base as a valued facility. The last BOAC crossing by Boeing 314A was made from Poole to Baltimore on 7 March 1946.

Gradually the B314s departed Pan Am's fleet and found their way into the hands of charter operators or were sold for parts. The *California Clipper* was scrapped in 1950, as was the *American Clipper* and the *Dixie Clipper*. The *Pacific Clipper* was badly damaged by a storm and had to be salvaged for parts as did the *Atlantic Clipper*. The longest lasting B314 perhaps was the *Anzac Clipper,* which continued to fly in different hands until it was destroyed at Baltimore in 1951.

While it had undergone many trials and tribulations in its brief history, Pan American was now flying again, in charge of its own affairs. Trippe was back also as chairman and chief executive and he was using again the services of his old friend Lindbergh, who would be a board member until he retired in May 1974. Trippe was at the helm once more of the airline he had built from a small mailplane-carrying operation to a global airline now carrying 380,000 passengers annually and flying 359 million revenue passenger miles (575 million rpkm). The total operating revenue for the year 1945 was $69.3 million and the net profit from this revenue was $7.6 million.

Trippe was there to deal with competitors such as American Overseas Airlines, and when American Airlines returned to US shores to concentrate solely on American domestic services, the principal US competition would come from Trans World Airlines.

Trippe led the airline for another 23 years, until he retired on 7 May 1968, although he continued to attend board meetings until 1975. In 1968 he handed over the chairmanship of Pan Am (now Pan American World Airways) to Harold Gray and nominated Najeeb Halaby, former head of the Federal Aviation Administration, as president and chief operating officer. Shrewd as ever perhaps, Trippe retired one year before the airline experienced the first in a series of substantial and on-going financial losses, this time largely brought about by the heavy commitment to yet another remarkable aircraft fleet, this time the Boeing 747s.

The Jumbo 747s would make their impact upon a world now used to air travel – but no one would ever forget the Pan Am Clipper flying-boats.

Appendix – Aircraft Data

SIKORSKY S-38A

Type	Amphibian	
Wing span	72ft	21.8m
Length	40ft	12.1m
Height	14ft	4.2m
Gross weight	9,200lb	4,182kg
Capacity	3 crew	8 passengers
Engines	Two Pratt & Whitney Wasps developing 450hp each	
Cruising speed	110mph	176kmh
Range	600st ml	960km
Fuel capacity	330gals	1500lt
Service ceiling	20,000ft	6060m

A higher gross weight model the S-38B had slightly more powerful P & W engines.

CONSOLIDATED COMMODORE

Type	Flying-boat	
Wing span	100ft	30m
Length	68ft	21m
Height	16ft	5m
Gross weight	17,650lb	8022kg
Capacity	4 crew	22 passengers
Engines	Two Pratt & Whitney Hornets developing 575hp each	
Cruising speed	100mph	161kmh
Range	1000st ml	1600km
Fuel capacity	650 US gals	2950lt
Service ceiling	11,250ft	3400m

SIKORSKY S-40

Type	Flying-boat	
Wing span	114ft	35m
Length	77ft	23.5m
Height	24ft	7.3m
Gross weight	34,000lb	15,436kg
Capacity	5 crew	40 passengers
Engines	Four Pratt & Whitney Hornets developing 575hp each	
Cruising speed	120mph	194kmh
Range	900st ml	1440km
Fuel capacity	1040gals	4763lt
Service ceiling	13,000ft	3940m

SIKORSKY S-42

Type	Flying-boat	
Wing span	114ft	34.7m
Length	69ft	20.9m
Height	17ft	5.1m
Gross weight	39,000lb	17,700kg
Capacity	5 crew	38 passengers
Engines	Four Pratt & Whitney Hornets developing 700hp each	
Cruising speed	150mph	240kmh
Range	750ml	1200km
Fuel capacity	1240gals	5636lt
Service ceiling	16,000ft	4850m

Note: The first three of Pan Am's S-40s were standard models and the following four S-42As, of 40,000lb gross weight and 750-hp engines. The remaining three S-42Bs had a 42,000lb MTOW and slightly higher cruising speed.

MARTIN M-130

Type	Flying-boat	
Wing span	130ft	39.3m
Length	91ft	27.7m
Height	25ft	7.6m
Gross weight	52,250lb	23,750kg
Capacity	7 crew	44 passengers
Engines	Four Pratt & Whitney Twin Wasps developing 830hp each	
Cruising speed	160mph	256kmh
Range	3,200st ml	5150km
Fuel capacity	4000gals	18,160lt
Service ceiling	20,000ft	6060m

BOEING 314

Type	Flying-boat	
Wing span	152ft	36m
Length	106ft	32m
Height	28ft	8,48m
Gross weight	82,500lb	37,500kg
Capacity	9–10 crew	74 passengers
Engines	Four Wright Double Cyclones developing 1500hp each	
Cruising speed	150mph	240kmh
Range	3500ml	5600km
Fuel capacity	4200gals	19,070lt
Service ceiling	13.400ft	4060m

Note: *The Boeing 314A model offered a fuel capacity increase of 1200gals and uprated engines of 1600hp.*

WATER-BASED AIRCRAFT USED BY PAN AMERICAN

Model	Type	Number employed	Remarks
Fairchild FC-2	Wheels or floats	One chartered; further six later acquired	Used only by subsidiary or affiliates
Sikorsky S-36	Amphibian	One leased from manufacturer	
Sikorsky S-38	Amphibian	38 bought; one extra	According to PAA records delivered but crashed
Consolidated Commodore	Flying-boat	14 acquired	
Sikorsky S-40	Flying-boat	Three bought	
Sikorsky S-41	Amphibian	Three bought	Used by subsidiaries
Sikorsky S-42	Flying-boat	10	
Sikorsky S-43	Amphibian	12	Three used by Pan Am; rest by subsidiaries
Douglas Dolphin	Amphibian	Two	Used only by CNAC China
Martin M-130	Flying-boat	Three bought	
Boeing 314	Flying-boat	12	Nine used by Pan Am; three by BOAC

Bibliography

BOOKS

Airlines of the United States Since 1914, R. E. G. Davies, Putnam, 1972

An American Saga: Juan Trippe and his Pan American Empire, Robert Daley, Random House, NY, 1980

The Aspirin Age, Isabel Leighton, The Bodley Head, 1950

The Aviation Careers of Igor Sikorsky, University of Washington Press, 1989

Boeing Aircraft Since 1916, Peter M. Bowers, Putnam, 1989

Britain's Imperial Air Routes, 1918 to 1939, Robin Higham, G. T. Foulis & Co, 1960

Empires of the Sky, Anthony Sampson, Hodder & Stoughton Ltd, 1984

The History of BOAC, Winston Bray, BOAC, 1974

A History of the World's Airlines, R. E. G. Davies, Oxford University Press, 1964

Jane's All the World's Aircraft, Sampson, Low and Marston, London, 1935, 1936

Jane's 100 Significant Aircraft, H. F. King, Jane's, 1970

Lockheed Aircraft Since 1913, Rene J. Francillon, Putnam, 1982

Major Airports of the World, 1979 and 1983, Roy Allen, Ian Allan Ltd, London

Pictorial History of Pan American World Airways, P. St John Turner, Ian Allan Ltd, 1973

Raise Heaven and Earth: the story of Martin Marietta people and their achievements, William B. Harwood, Simon and Schuster, 1993

The Second World War, Winston S. Churchill, Cassell, 1959

Shorts Aircraft since 1900, C. H. Barnes, Putnam, 1967

Shorts the Planemakers, Jane's Publishing Co, 1984

The Technical Development of Modern Aviation, R. Miller and D. Sawers, Routledge and Kegan Paul, 1968

Wings Across the World, Harald Penrose, Cassell, 1980

Wings to the Orient, Stan Cohen from Aardvark Books, Westbury, Wiltshire, UK, 1994

World Airline Record, 7th edition, Roadcap & Associates, 1972

REPORTS, DOCUMENTATION AND MAGAZINE ARTICLES

Pan American World Airways Annual Reports

'Ocean Air Transport', 29th annual Wilbur Wright Memorial Lecture, by Juan Trippe, Royal Aeronautical Society, 1941

'Pan American Airways', Wesley Phillips Newton, *The Encyclopedia of American Business History and Biography,* Fax-on-File Inc, NY, 1992

'Charles A. Lindbergh', Juan Trippe, The Wings Club 1977 Sight Lecture

'Pan Am's Pacific', Henry Scammell, *Air & Space* magazine, September 1989

'The Boeing 314 Clipper: the flying hotel that went to war', Boeing Historical Archives, 1987

'Britain's Overseas Territories', Foreign & Commonwealth Office, 1999

'Flying-boats and Air Transport', David West, *Aeronautics* magazine, October 1956

'Aquila Airways: Britain's only flying-boat operator', Roy Allen, *Aeronautics* magazine, November 1956

'Design trends in water-based aircraft', John D. Pierson, *Aeronautics* magazine, January 1957

Index